COOPERATIVE LEARNING

COOPERATIVE LEARNING

Dr. Reena Agarwal
and
Nandita Nagar

KALPAZ

Cooperative Learning

ISBN: 978-81-7835-863-5

Published in 2011 in India by
Kalpaz Publications
C-30, Satyawati Nagar,
Delhi-110052
E-mail: kalpaz@hotmail.com
Phone : 9212729499

Lasser Type Setting by: Rudra Computer Graphics, Delhi
Printed at : Chawla Offset Press, Delhi

Contents

Preface

Cooperative Learning can be regarded as a philosophy and not just a classroom technique. In all situations where people come together in groups, it suggests a way of dealing with people which respects and highlights individual group member's abilities and contributions. The underlying premise of cooperative learning is based upon consensus building through cooperation by group members in contrast to competition in which individuals out rule other group members. Cooperative learning as a philosophy can be applied in the classroom, at committee meetings, with community groups and generally as a way of living with and dealing with other people.

This act of cooperation is something which is deeply embedded in our society. It seems to be a fundamental aspect of our everyday lives. Right from birth until death, cooperation forms the base of our lives. The society of man has survived because the cooperativeness of its members made survival possible. People cooperate for external rewards; they cooperate in order to form and further relationships and they cooperate in order to share the activities they are involved in. If we view learning situations as part of the wider social context in which we live, then it is not difficult to relate to this. Although our education system is less concerned and many a times overlooks fostering cooperation in learning but informally learners do work together, cooperate and share their learning. Formalizing what happens informally is one of the purposes of Cooperative Learning.

Hence, keeping this in view, the present book has been written with the objective to give a holistic view of the concept of cooperative learning to the readers and to make them familiar with the art of using cooperative learning methods and strategies in their classroom teaching. It is hoped that the humble effort made in the form of this book will assist in the accomplishment of bringing about a qualitative change in education at all levels.

Regarding the organization, the book consists of ten chapters, well arranged in a coherent manner. Chapter One deals primarily with the three different learning patterns found in any educational setting namely- competitive, individualistic and cooperative learning. It includes the description of all the three learning patterns, how they are structured and what are their outcomes. It points towards the over emphasis of competitive learning structure in our classrooms and draws attention towards its drawbacks, and at the same time explains the importance of cooperation in learning and its inculcation in the present day educational system. Chapter Two presents an overview of Cooperative learning supported by its historical background. Theoretical basis of cooperative learning which have guided research on cooperative learning viz.- Social Interdependence theory, Cognitive development theory or Constructivism and Behaviour approach have been discussed at length separately in the successive chapters Chapter Three, Four and Five respectively. Chapter Six presents a detail account of methods/strategies of Cooperative learning and their implementation. Chapter Seven focuses on the procedure for structuring Cooperative learning in the classroom. Chapter Eight highlights the benefits of Cooperative learning equally focusing on academic, social and psychological benefits. Chapter Nine revolves around the teacher's role and concerns in Cooperative learning. Chapter Ten exhaustively deals with the need of Cooperative learning in present times.

This book is primarily intended to serve as a reference book for graduate, post graduate and M.Phil students of Education of various Universities. It is hoped that the book shall provide guidelines to all interested research scholars as well. The book is, in fact, an outgrowth of our experience and learning and working on cooperative learning for the last few years.

We shall feel amply rewarded if the book proves helpful to scholars and educators in their attempt to focus on Cooperative learning. We value reader's feedback and we look forward to their suggestions to make this important work successful.

Dr. Reena Agarwal

Nandita Nagar

1

Competitive, Individualistic and Cooperative Learning

In our education system the beliefs or concerns about the impact of teacher-student and student-materials interaction are as high and prevalent as concerns about the 3R's- reading, writing and arithmetic. The teacher-student and student-materials interaction in instructional situations have received extensive attention in teacher pre-service and in-service training. These two types of interactions, however, are not the only forms of interaction within instructional situations. The interaction that most influences students' performance in instructional situations is student-student interaction.

How students interact with each other depends primarily on the type of interdependence the teacher structures among students learning goals and this in turn largely determines the cognitive and affective outcomes of instruction.

In the present times, how students perceive each other and interact with one another is a neglected aspect of instruction. Much training time is devoted to helping teachers arrange appropriate interactions between students and materials (i.e. text books, curriculum programs) and some time is spent on how teachers should interact with students, but how students should interact with one another is relatively ignored. It should not be. How teachers structure student-student interaction patterns has a lot to say about how well students learn, how they feel about school and the teacher, how they feel about each other and how much self esteem they have. So, it is essential and imperative that all teachers need to know and understand the instructional skill of how and when to structure students learning goals.

In any educational setting, the pattern in which students learn and interact can be structured in three different ways-

1. COMPETITIVE LEARNING- In this type of learning, students work against each other to achieve a goal that only one or few students can attain. Students are graded on a curve, which requires them to work faster and more accurately than their peers. Student's goal achievements are negatively correlated with each other to cause negative interdependence and oppositional interaction. Thus, students seek an outcome that is personally beneficial but detrimental to others with whom they are competitively linked.

For example in a spelling test, the student who gets the maximum spellings correct is ranked first in the class.

2. INDIVIDUALISTIC LEARNING- In this type of learning, students work by themselves to accomplish learning goals unrelated to those of others. Individual goals are assigned each day, students efforts are evaluated on a fixed set of standards and rewards are given accordingly. There is no communication among students for joint attainment of goals and hence, due to lack of interdependence, an absence of interaction is often marked. Whether or not a student accomplishes the goal has no influence on whether other students achieve their goals. Thus, a student seeks an outcome that is personally beneficial and ignores the goal achievement of other students as irrelevant. For example, in a spelling test, when students work on their own, any student who correctly spells 90 percent or more words passes.

3. COOPERATIVE LEARNING- In this type of learning, the students work together to accomplish shared goals. In this situation, students work cooperatively with a vested interest in others learning as their own. Their goal achievements are positively correlated with others to cause positive interdependence and promotive interaction. Thus, students seek outcomes that are beneficial to all those with whom they are cooperatively linked. For example, to prepare for the spelling test, students work together in small groups to help each other learn the words in order to take the spelling test individually on another day. Each students score on the test is increased by bonus points if the group is successful (i.e. the groups total meets specified criteria).

In an ideal classroom all the three learning patterns should be appropriately used. All students should learn how to work cooperatively with others, compete for fun and enjoyment and work on their own. No aspect of teaching is more important than the appropriate use of different learning patterns. But, unfortunately, most students perceive school as predominantly competitive enterprises as for the past half-century, competitive and individualistic learning patterns have dominated our education system. Competitive and individualistic learning situations instill in learners such value systems which form a part of the hidden curriculum beneath the surface of school life i.e. when students are exposed to such learning, they unknowingly, indirectly, involuntarily acquire such values which are not a part of the real school curriculum to be followed for the all round development of the students.

Whenever students engage in competitive efforts, for example, they learn the values of-

(a) Commitment to getting more than others (there is a built-in concern that one is smarter, faster, stronger, more competent, and more successful than others so that one will win and others will lose),

(b) Success depends on beating, defeating and getting more than other people (triumphing over others and being 'Number One' are valued),

(c) What is important is winning, not mastery or excellence,

(d) Opposing, obstructing, and sabotaging the success of others is a natural way of life (winning depends on a good offence-doing better than others- and a good defense-not letting anyone do better than you),

(e) Feeling joy and pride in one's wins and other's losses (the pleasure of winning is associated with other's disappointment with losing),

(f) Other's are a threat to one's success,

(g) A person's worth (own and other's) is conditional and contingent on his or her 'wins', (a persons worth is never fixed, it depends on the latest victory),

(h) Winning not learning, is the goal of academic work, and

(i) People who are different are to be either feared (if they have an advantage) or held in contempt (if they have a handicap).

The values which students inherently learn when they are exposed to Individualistic experiences are-

(a) Commitment to one's own self interest (only personal success is viewed as important, other's success is irrelevant),

(b) Success depends on one's own efforts,

(c) The pleasure of succeeding is personal and relevant to only oneself,

(d) Other people are irrelevant,

(e) Self-worth is based on a one-dimensional view that the characteristics that help the person succeed are valued (in school that is primarily reading and math ability),

(f) Extrinsic motivation to gain rewards for achieving up to criteria is valued, and

(g) Similar people are liked and dissimilar people are disliked.

In contrast to these, the values inherently taught by Cooperative efforts are-

(a) Commitment to own and other's success and well being as well as to the common good,

(b) Success depends on joint efforts to achieve mutual goals,

(c) Facilitating, promoting, and encouraging the success of others is a natural way of life (a smart cooperator will always find ways to promote, facilitate, and encourage the efforts of others), the pleasure of succeeding is associated with other's happiness in their success,

(d) Other people are potential contributor to one's success,

(e) Own and other people's worth is unconditional (because there are so many diverse ways that a person may contribute to a joint effort, everyone has value all the time),

(f) Intrinsic motivation based on striving to learn, grow, develop and succeed is valued (learning is the goal, not winning),

(g) People who are different from oneself are to be valued as they can make unique contributions to the joint effort.

Nevertheless, each learning pattern has its place. In an ideal classroom, all the three learning patterns/ experiences-competitive, individualistic and cooperative are to be used. This does not mean, however that they should all be used equally or the dominant one should out rule the rest. The basic foundation of instruction, the underlying context on which all instruction rests is cooperation. Unless used within a context of cooperation, competitive and individualistic instructions lose much of their effectiveness. Extensive use of Competitive and Individualistic learning experiences instead of promoting positive development of the child, can negatively affect his or her psychological health. Cooperation is like a forest cover and competition and individualism are like individual trees. Competitive and individualistic learning should be used to supplement and enrich the basic cooperation among students. It is apparent that when the three different learning patterns are used appropriately and in an integrated way, the combination is far more powerful than any one of them employed separately.

COOPERATION IN LEARNING

The act of cooperation is something which is deeply embedded in our society. It seems to be a fundamental aspect of our everyday lives. Right from birth until death, cooperation forms the base of our lives. The society of man has survived because the cooperativeness of its members made survival possible. People cooperate for external rewards; they cooperate in order to form and further relationships and they cooperate in order to share the activities they are involved in. If we view learning situations as part of the wider social context in which we live, then it is not difficult to relate to this. Although our education system is less concerned and many a times overlooks fostering cooperation in learning but informally learners do work together, cooperate and share their learning. In a typical classroom, a teacher can be heard saying, "Work individually". "Do not peep in your partner's copy". "Do not talk in the class". "Let Ramesh answer the question, do not prompt him from the back", many a times. But what about the homework assignment the children are given? They discuss their answers over telephones, cell phones, and at times a group of friends hang out at one person's place and jointly complete the assignment to be submitted the next day for grading. How so ever strict a painting teacher may be, giving instructions to students to bring their own colours to class, but if one of the student forgets to bring them or they fall off his bag on his way to school, within seconds his colour box gets ready. This all is done by the students to save their classmate from punishment, from disqualification and from losing or getting failed. This act of generosity of classmates somewhere lays down the foundation of development and strengthening of social relationships. When a student is given a certain topic to decorate the weekly notice board in class, a bag full of creative ideas, any type of help, materials etc pour out and the friends of the student try to effectively manage things and give their best to help their friend prepare for the task.

All this and more, the students do, because they enjoy the shared or joint activities, they try to develop friendship and also to achieve shared goals. They also know that it is beneficial for them and for others to share their learning.

Formalizing what happens informally is one of the purposes of Cooperative Learning.

2

Overview of Cooperative Learning

Cooperative Learning offers a view of learning which is socially based. In the very broadest sense, cooperative learning involves working together on some task or issue in a way that promotes individual learning through process of collaboration in groups. It is "the opportunity to learn through the expression and exploration of diverse ideas and experiences in cooperative company. It is not about competing with fellow members of the group and winning, but about using the diverse resources available in the group to deepen understanding, sharpen judgement and extend knowledge." (*Cowie* and *Rudduck*, 1988, p.30).

Cooperative Learning is process driven, i.e. those involved engage in a social process and have to pay attention to that process in order for them to achieve their desired end point. It usually involves people working in groups (at least two people are involved, usually more). There may be "group products" towards which learners are working and there may be "individual products" which are achieved through the people in the group helping each other deal with their own individual learning concerns. Cooperative learning can give rise to products which are not easily achievable by people learning on their own. Because cooperative learning has a large social dimension to it, it is usually enjoyable and developmental i.e. it gives rise to outcomes which are not only purely academic but also social and psychological such as increased competence in working with others, self assurance, personal insight and so on which are an equally important and integral part of child's personality and his positive all round development.

Nelson –Le Gall (1992) captures the nature of cooperative learning when she states "Learning and understanding are not merely individual processes supported by the social context, rather they are the result of a continuous, dynamic negotiation between the individual and the social setting in which the individual's activity takes place. Both the individual and social context are active and constructive in producing learning and understanding". (p. 52).

Cooperative learning can be regarded as a philosophy and not just a classroom technique. In all situations where people come together in groups, it suggests a way of dealing with people which respects and highlights individual group member's abilities and contributions. The underlying premise of cooperative learning is based upon consensus building through cooperation by group members in contrast to competition in which individuals out rule other group members. Cooperative learning as a philosophy can be applied in the classroom, at committee meetings, with community groups and generally as a way of living with and dealing with other people.

2.1 DEFINITION OF COOPERATIVE LEARNING

Cooperative Learning can be defined as a structured, systematic, instructional strategy in which small groups work together towards a common goal. Cooperative learning is a relatively new concept and is considered as having the potential of improving education, regardless of the discipline or level of instruction.

Some recent definitions of Cooperative Learning include-

An activity involving a small group of learners who work together as a team to solve a problem, complete a task, or accomplish a common goal. (*Artzt* and *Newman* 1990)

A task for group discussion and resolution (if possible), requiring face-to-face interaction, an atmosphere of cooperation and mutual helpfulness, and individual accountability. (*Davidson* 1990).

Spencer Kagan (1990) provided an excellent definition of cooperative learning by looking at general structures which can be applied to any situation. He defined cooperative learning as the structural approach to cooperative learning which is based on the creation, analysis and systematic application of structures or content-free ways of organizing social interaction in the classroom. Structures usually involve a series of steps, with prescribed behaviour at each step. Structures may be used repeatedly with almost any subject matter, at a wide range of grade levels and at various points in a lesson plan.

Cooperative learning also falls in the more general category of "collaborative learning," which is described as working in groups of two or more, mutually searching for understanding, solutions, or meanings, or creating a product. (*Goodsell*, *Maher*, and *Tinto* 1992).

Johnson and Johnson and Holubec have also given a working definition of cooperative learning. According to *Johnson & Johnson and Holubec* (1998, p.5) **"Cooperative Learning is the instructional use of small groups through which**

students work together to maximize their own and each others learning". In classrooms where Cooperative Learning is practiced, students pursue learning in groups of varying size, negotiating, initiating, planning and evaluating together. Rather than working as individuals in competition with every other individual in the classroom, students are given the responsibility of creating a learning community where all students participate in significant and meaningful ways. Students use a variety of learning activities to improve their understanding of a subject. Each member of a team or group is responsible not only for learning what is taught, but also for helping teammates to learn, thus creating an atmosphere of achievement. Students work through the assignments until all group members successfully understand and complete it.

2.2 ESSENTIAL ELEMENTS OF COOPERATIVE LEARNING

There are five fundamental elements involved in Cooperative Learning. These are -

(i) **Positive Interdependence** - means the group has a clear task or goal so everyone knows that they have to sink or swim together. The efforts of any person extend benefit not only to that individual, but everyone else in the group. The key to positive interdependence is having commitments made to personal success as well as the success of every member of the group.

(ii) **Individual and Group Accountability** - means the group is accountable for achieving its goals and each member must be accountable for contributing a fair share of the work towards the group goal. No one can "hitch hike" on the work of others. The performance of each individual must be assessed and the results given back to the group.

(iii) **Interpersonal and Small Group Skills** - interpersonal and small group skills are required to function as a part of a group. These are basic teamwork skills. Group members must know how to and be motivated to provide effective leadership, make decisions, build trust, communicate and manage conflicts.

(iv) **Face-to-Face Promotive Interaction** - means that students promote each others success by sharing of resources. They help, support, encourage and praise each others efforts to learn. Both academic and personal supports are part of this mutual goal.

(v) **Group Processing** - group members need to feel free to communicate openly with each other to express concerns as well as to celebrate accomplishments. They should discuss how well they are achieving their goals and maintaining effective working relationships.

2.3 DIFFERENCE BETWEEN COOPERATIVE LEARNING GROUPS AND TRADITIONAL LEARNING GROUPS

At this point, it is important also to consider what cooperative learning is not. According to *Johnson et al* (1991), having students sit side-by-side at the same table and talk with each other as they do their individual assignments, having students do a task individually with instructions that those who finish first are to help the slower students, or assigning a report to a group where one student does all the work and the others put their names on it is not Cooperative Learning. Putting students into groups does not necessarily gain a cooperative relationship, it has to be structured and managed by the teacher.

There are a number of differences between the typical uses of classroom learning groups and cooperative learning groups. These differences are-

1. Cooperative learning groups are based on positive interdependence among group members, in which goals are structured so that students need to be concerned about the performance of all group members as well as their own.

2. In cooperative learning groups, there is a clear individual accountability such that each student's mastery of the assigned material is assessed, each student is given feedback on his or her progress, and the group is given feedback on how each member is progressing so that other group members know whom to help and encourage. In traditional learning groups, individual students are not often held individually accountable for providing their share of the group's work, and occasionally students will 'hitchhike' on the work of others.

3. In cooperative learning groups, the membership is typically heterogeneous in ability and personal characteristics; traditional learning groups are often homogenous in membership.

4. In cooperative learning groups, all members share responsibility for performing leadership actions in the group. In traditional learning groups, a leader is often appointed and put in charge of the group.

5. In cooperative learning groups, responsibility for each other's learning is shared. Group members are expected to provide help and encouragement to each other in order to ensure that all members do the assigned work. In traditional learning groups, members are seldom held responsible for each other's learning.

6. In cooperative learning groups, student's goals focus on bringing each members learning to the maximum and on

maintaining good working relationships among members. In traditional classroom learning groups, students most often focus only on completing the assignment.

7. In cooperating learning groups, the social skills students need in order to work collaboratively (such as leadership, ability to communicate, to trust one another, and manage conflict) are taught directly. In traditional classroom learning groups, interpersonal and small-group skills are assumed- most often mistakenly.

8. When cooperative learning groups are used, the teacher observes the groups, analyzes the problems they have working together, and gives feedback to each group on how well they are managing the group task. Teacher observation and intervention seldom take place in traditional learning groups.

Table 2.1

Differences between Cooperative Learning Groups and Traditional Learning Groups

Cooperative Learning Groups	*Traditional Learning Groups*
Positive interdependence	No interdependence
Individual accountability	No individual accountability
Heterogeneous	Homogenous
Shared leadership	One appointed leader
Shared responsibility for each other	Responsibility only for self
Task and maintenance emphasized	Only task emphasized
Social skills directly taught	Social skills assumed and ignored
Teacher observes and intervenes	Teacher ignores group functioning
Groups process their effectiveness	No group processing

9. In cooperative learning, the teacher structures procedures for groups to "process" how effectively they are working. In traditional group learning situations, no attention is given to the way the group is working or not working.

The differences between the cooperative learning groups and traditional learning groups can be summarized as under-

2.4 TYPES OF COOPERATIVE LEARNING GROUPS

Johnson, Johnson, and *Holubec* (1998) have identified three types of cooperative learning groups- formal, informal, and base groups.

Formal cooperative learning groups range in length from one class period to several weeks. The teacher can structure any academic assignment or course requirement for formal cooperative learning. Formal cooperative learning groups ensure that students are actively involved in the intellectual work of organizing material, explaining it, summarizing it, and integrating it into existing conceptual structures. They are the heart of using cooperative learning.

Informal cooperative learning groups are ad-hoc groups that may last from a few minutes to a whole class period. The teacher uses them during direct teaching (lectures, demonstrations) to focus student attention on the material to be learned, set a mood conducive to learning, help set expectations about material, what the lesson will cover, ensure that students are cognitively processing the material being taught, and provide closure to an instructional session.

Cooperative base groups are long term (lasting for at least a year), heterogeneous groups with stable membership whose primary purpose is for members to give each other the support, help, encouragement, and assistance each needs to progress academically. Base groups provide students with long-term, committed relationships.

2.5 HISTORICAL BACKGROUND OF COOPERATIVE LEARNING

Cooperative learning has been around for a very long time. *Slavin* (1995) pointed out that the history of cooperative learning can be traced back as far as in the 17th century. *Comenius* in the 17th century believed that students would benefit both by teaching and being taught by other students. *Rousseau* in the 18th century recognized a collective 'general will' which represents the common good among people and promotes liberty, equality and fraternity among people. He also believed that individuals must be encouraged to reason their way through to their own conclusions, they should not rely on the authority of the teacher. Thus, instead of being taught other people's ideas, Emile' was encouraged to draw his own conclusions from his own experiences. *Pestalozzi* in the 19th century was against rote memory and cramming of subject matter. He wished that a child should himself search out knowledge and develop self-reliance. He emphasized observation and study according to psychology and advocated that a child should experience things and explain them in his own words. In this way, he followed Rousseau in emphasizing oral education and gaining real knowledge of things and material objects by his own efforts, observation and experiences. He advocated self-discipline through love, sympathy and human feeling and also a new pupil-teacher relationship. *John Dewey* in the 20th century held some form of cooperation among students as essential to learning. Group learning was a prominent component of John Dewey's experiential classroom.

Thus, concept of cooperative learning is not new in education. Although the term may not have been used, cooperative learning in some form has been happening for decades.

In the late 1930's however, interpersonal competition began to be emphasized in schools and in the late 1960's, individualistic learning began to be used extensively. Following this, research on cooperative learning gained momentum in 1970's when *David Johnson* and *Roger Johnson* at University of Minneapolis started training teachers in Cooperative Learning. In mid 1970s *Robert Slavin* began development of cooperative curricula and *Spencer Kagan* continued research on cooperation among children. *Shlomo Sharan* and *Yael Sharan*, *Elliot Aronson*, *Elizabeth Cohen*, all worked on the approach but it was in early 1990s that Cooperative Learning gained popularity among educators and it was in 1996 that First Annual Cooperative Learning Conference was held at Minneapolis.

A partial timeline of the history of cooperative learning can be illustrated as follows-

Table 2.2
Timeline of the History of Cooperative Learning

DATE	*EVENT*
Early 1900s	John Dewey, Kurt Lewin, Jean Piaget, Lev Vygotsky
1960s	
1960s	Stuart Cook: Research on cooperationMadsen (Kagan): Research on cooperation and competition in children Bruner, Suchman: Inquiry (Discovery) Learning Movement B.F. Skinner: Programmed Learning, behaviour modification
1962	Morton Deutsch (Nebraska Symposium): Cooperation and trust, conflict Robert Blake and Jane Mouton: research on inter group competition
1966-1969	David Johnson, U of MN: Begins training teachers in Cooperative Learning Roger Johnson: Joins David at U of MN

(Contd.)

(Contd. Table)

DATE	*EVENT*
1970s	
1970	David Johnson: Social Psychology of Education
1973	David DeVries and Keith Edwards: Combined instructional games approach with inter group competition, teams- games-tournament
1974-1975	David and Roger Johnson: Research review on cooperation/competitionDavid and Roger Johnson: Learning Together and Alone
Mid 1970s	Annual Symposium at APA (David DeVries and Keith Edwards, David and Roger Johnson, Stuart Cook, Elliot Aronson, Elizabeth Cohen, others) Robert Slavin: Begins development of cooperative curricula Spencer Kagan: Continued research on cooperation among children
1976	Shlomo and Yael Sharan: Small group Teaching (Group Investigation)
1978	Elliot Aronson: Jigsaw Classroom, Journal of Research and Development in Education, (Cooperation Issue)
1980s	
1981,1983	David and Roger Johnson: Meta-analysis of research on cooperation
1985	Elizabeth Cohen: Designing Group work Spencer Kagan: Developed structures approach to cooperative learning
1989	David and Roger Johnson: Cooperation and Competition- Theory and Research
1990s	
Early 1990s	Cooperative learning gains popularity among educators

(Contd.)

(Contd. Table)

DATE	*EVENT*
1996	First Annual Cooperative Learning Leadership Conference, Minneapolis.

3

Social Interdependence Theory And It's Impact on Cooperative Learning

Social interdependence theory is based on the premise that the way in which social interdependence is structured determines how individuals interact and that determines outcomes. *Koffka, Kurt Lewin* and *Morton Deutsch* are the main proponents of this theory. The theory assumes that cooperative efforts are based on intrinsic motivation generated by interpersonal factors in working together and joint aspirations to achieve a significant goal.

Table 3.1
Social Interdependence Theory: History of Theory and Research

Premise:	The way in which social interdependence is structured determines hour individuals interact with and that determines outcomes.

Early 1900s	Kurt Koffka: Groups are dynamic wholes featuring member interdependence
1920-1940	Kurt Lewin: Interdependence among members, common goals
1940s-1970s	Morton Deutsch: Positive, negative, and no goal interdependence (cooperative, competitive, individualistic efforts); two mediating variables (trust and conflict); distributive justice
1960s	David and Roger Johnson: Impact of social interdependence on achievement, relationships, psychological health and social development, mediating variables (positive interdependence, individual accountability, promotive interaction, social skills, group processing)
1970s	Dean Tjosvold: Research in business and industry setting

Assumptions of social interdependence theory:

1. Cooperative efforts are based on intrinsic motivation generated by interpersonal factors in working together and joint aspirations to achieve a significant goal

2. Focus on relational concepts dealing with what happens among individuals

Social interdependence theory provides us with a conceptual framework for understanding how cooperative learning may be-

(a) fruitfully structured
(b) adapted to a wide variety of instructional situations and
(c) applied to a wide range of issues.

Theorizing on social interdependence began in the early 1900s, when one of the founders of the Gestalt school of psychology, *Kurt Koffka*, proposed that groups were dynamic wholes in which the interdependence among members could vary. *Kurt Lewin* refined *Koffka's* notions in the 1920s and 1930s. *Kurt Lewin's* theory served as the primary foundation on which subsequent research and discussion of cooperative learning is based.

3.1 Kurt Lewin's Learning Theory and its Impact on Cooperative Learning

Kurt Lewin gave his theory of learning which is commonly known as Kurt Lewin's Field Theory. In his field theory, a 'field' is defined as 'the totality of coexisting facts which are conceived of as mutually interdependent', individuals are seem to behave differently according to the way in which tensions between perceptions of the self and the environment are worked through. In order to understand behaviour, it is necessary to view the whole psychological field or 'life space' within which people act. Within this individuals and groups can be seen in topological terms (using map like representations). Individuals participate in a series of life spaces (such as the family, school, work etc.) and these all are constructed under the influence of various force vectors.

Kurt Lewin also looked to the power of underlying forces (needs) to determine behaviour and hence, expressed a preference for psychological descriptions of the field as opposed to physical or physiological. Thus, in Lewin's theory, we can see that he drew together insights from topology (eg. life space), psychology (need, aspiration, etc.), and sociology (eg. force fields-motives clearly being dependent on group pressures). These three aspects of his thoughts are inseparable and comprise a single well-integrated system.

Kurt Lewin's theory had a profound impact on a generation of researchers and thinkers concerned with group dynamics.

Two key ideas emerged out of field theory that are crucial to an appreciation of group process- interdependence of fate and task interdependence.

Interdependence of fate- Groups come into being in a psychological sense, not because their members necessarily are similar to one another (although they may be); rather, a group exists when people in it realize that their fate depends on the fate of the group as a whole.

Kurt Lewin was of the view that during the formation of a group, it is not similarity or dissimilarity of individuals that constitute a group, but rather interdependence of fate. Any normal group, and certainly any developed and organized one contains and should contain individuals of very different character. This helps individuals become more tolerant of differences of opinion and once a person realizes that much of his own fate depends upon the fate of his entire group, the person becomes ready and even eager to take over a fair share of responsibility for the group's welfare.

Task interdependence- Besides interdependence of fate, another significant factor Lewin advocated was interdependence in the goals of group members. If the group task is such that members of the group are dependent on each other for achievement, then a powerful dynamic is created. These implications can be positive or negative. In the former case, one person's success either directly facilitates other's success or indirectly is necessary for other's to succeed. In negative interdependence-known more usually as competition- one person's success is another's failure.

Kurt Lewin also put forth the argument that people may come to a group with very different dispositions, but if they share a common objective, they are likely to act together to achieve it. This links back to what is usually described as Lewin's field theory. He also explained that an intrinsic state of tension within group members stimulates or motivates movement towards the achievement of desired common goals. Interdependence (of fate and task) also results in the group being a dynamic whole. This means that a change in one member or sub groups impacts upon others.

Thus, we can summarize the important views or elements of Kurt Lewin's theory which formed the basis of cooperative learning as under-

(a) The essence of a group is the interdependence among members (created by common goals) which results in the group being a "dynamic whole" so that a change in the state of any member or sub group changes the state of any other member or sub group and,

(b) An intrinsic state of tension within group members motivates movement toward the accomplishment of the desired common goals.

Besides these two significant elements, *Kurt Lewin* also put forth other important elements which are also a part of basic foundation stone of cooperative learning. These are -

Democracy- *Lewin* admitted that democracy was far more difficult form of social structure to attain and to maintain than autocracy. *Lewin* explored the different styles or types of leadership on group structure and member behaviour and concluded that there was more originality, group-mindedness and friendliness in democratic groups than in autocratic or laissez-faire. This view is also in tandem with the view of type of atmosphere and leadership sought after or wanted in cooperative learning groups.

Kurt Lewin was also involved in leadership and group dynamics training. The participative groups which he trained were known as 'basic skill training groups' or T-groups. During the training sessions, he discovered that learning is best facilitated in an environment where there is dialectic tension and conflict between immediate, concrete and analytic detachment. The following elements of the T-group are particularly noteworthy with respect to the theoretical basis of cooperative learning-

Feedback- Feedback was broadly used to have the information or real knowledge about the desired and actual result. It was then used to describe the adjustment of a process.

Unfreezing- An environment was created in the group so that former values and beliefs could be challenged and individuals motivated to accept the change.

Participant Observation- Members of the group had to participate emotionally in the group as well as observe themselves and the group objectively.

The element of 'Group Processing' in cooperative learning can be said to have its roots somewhere in the above mentioned elements of Kurt Lewin's research.

Cognitive aids- *Lewin* entailed the provision of models or organizing ideas through the brief lectures, handouts, film clips or video. He advocated that use of such cognitive aids, lectures, reading assignments and theory sessions facilitated the learning of group members. The use of cognitive aids is considered as an integral preparatory part while organizing a cooperative learning lesson in a classroom.

Thus, we see that Kurt Lewin's theory, his views and suggestions have provided a wide base on which cooperative learning has been fruitfully structured.

3.2 Morton Deutsch's Theory of Cooperation and Competition and its Impact on Cooperative Learning

Morton Deutsch (1949), Lewin's student, extended Lewin's reasoning about social interdependence and formulated a theory of cooperation and competition. Deutsch's theory has served as a major conceptual structure for Cooperative Learning till date. Deutsch's theory was extended and applied to education by *Johnson* and *Johnson* (1970, 1974, and 1989) at the University of Minnesota while putting cooperative learning into practice.

Deutsch propounded that social interdependence exists when individuals share common goals and each individual's outcomes are affected by the actions of the others. It may be differentiated from social dependence (i.e., the outcomes of one person are affected by the actions of a second person but not vice versa) and social independence (i.e., individual's outcomes are unaffected by each other's actions).

There are two types of social interdependence: cooperative and competitive. The absence of social interdependence and dependence results in individualistic efforts.

When individuals take action there are three ways what they do may be related to the action of others. One's actions may promote the success of others, obstruct the success of others, or not have any effect at all on the success or failure of others. In other words, individuals may-

1. Work together cooperatively to accomplish shared learning goals (social interdependence). When a situation is structured cooperatively, individual's goal achievements are positively correlated; individuals perceive that they can reach their goals if and only if the others in the group also reach their goals. Thus, individuals seek outcomes that are beneficial to all those with whom they are cooperatively linked.

2. Work against each other to achieve a goal that only one or a few can attain. When a situation is structured competitively, individual's goal achievements are negatively correlated; each individual perceives that when one person achieves his or her goal, all others with whom he or she is competitively linked fail to achieve their goals. Thus, individuals seek an outcome that is personally beneficial but detrimental to all others in the group.

3. Work by one self to accomplish goals unrelated to the goals of others. When a situation is structured individualistically, there is no correlation among participant's goal attainments. Each individual perceives that he or she can reach his or her goal regardless of whether other individuals attain or do not attain their goals. Thus, individuals seek an outcome that is personally beneficial without the concern for the outcomes of others.

Thus, we can see that the type of interdependence structured in a situation determines how individuals interact with each other, which in turn, determines outcomes. The interaction effects can be summarized in the following manner-

Table 3.2
Social Interdependence Theory

Process	*Cooperative*	*Competitive*	*Individualistic*
Interdependence	Positive	Negative	None
Interaction Pattern	Promotive	Oppositional	None
Outcome 1	High Effort To Achieve	Low Effort To Achieve	Low Effort To Achieve
Outcome 2	Positive Relationships	Negative Relationships	No Relationships
Outcome 3	Psychological Health	Psychological Illness	Psychological Pathology

From the above table it is clear that positive interdependence tends to result in promotive interaction, negative interdependence tends to result in oppositional interaction, and no interdependence results in an absence of interaction.

Promotive interaction also tends to result in a wide variety of outcomes that may be included into the categories of high effort to achieve, positive relationships, and psychological health. Oppositional interaction tends to result in low effort to achieve by most students, negative relationships, and low psychological health and no interaction ends to result in low effort to achieve, an absence of relationships, and psychological pathology.

Depending on whether individuals promote or obstruct each other's goal accomplishments, there is **substitutability** (i.e., the actions of one person substitute for the actions of another), **cathexis** (i.e., the investment of psychological energy in objects and events outside of oneself), and **inducibility** (i.e., openness to influence). In competitive situations the actions of participants do not substitute for each other, participants negatively cathect to each other's effective actions, and inducibility is low. When there is no interaction, there is no substitutability, cathexis, or inducibility. Essentially, in cooperative situations the actions of participants substitute for each other, participants positively cathect to each other's effective actions, and there is high inducibility among participants.

Morton Deutsch held that social interdependence is a generic human phenomenon which has impact on many different outcomes simultaneously. Based on the social interdependence theory given by Deutsch and the different categories and interaction patterns prescribed by him, researchers over many years focused their work on comparisons and outcomes of cooperative, competitive and individualistic processes and focused on such diverse dependent variables as individual achievement and retention, group and organizational productivity, higher-level reasoning, moral reasoning, achievement motivation, intrinsic motivation, transfer of training and learning, job satisfaction, interpersonal attraction, social support, interpersonal affection and love, attitudes toward diversity, prejudice, self-esteem, personal causation and locus of control, attributions concerning success and failure, psychological health, social competencies, and many others.

A meta-analysis of all studies (*Johnson & Johnson*, 1989) found that the average person cooperating performed at about two-third a standard deviation above the average person learning within a competitive situation (effect size= 0.67) or individualistic situation (effect size= 0.64). When only studies with high internal validity were included in the analysis, the effect sizes were 0.88 and 0.61, respectively.

(Effect sized was the difference between treatments divided by the pooled standard deviation of the two groups).

Such optimistic, constructive and encouraging results about the role of positive interdependence in learning situations put this element into prime focus and it literally became the basic foundation stone of cooperative learning around which the basic essence of cooperative learning evolves.

4

Constructivism and Cooperative Learning

The **cognitive developmental** perspective or which has been lately termed as **constructivistic approach** is grounded in the work of *Jean Piaget* and *Lev Vygotsky*. Piagetian perspective suggests that when individual work together, socio-cognitive conflict occurs and creates cognitive disequilibrium that stimrulates perspective taking ability (ability to understand how a situation appears to other people) and reasoning. *Vygotsky's* theory presents knowledge as a societal product and emphasizes over the importance of discussion and problem solving among peers.

The cognitive developmental theory states that children and adolescents continuously construct intelligence as they operate and discover their world. It is also known as 'Constructivism'. It is greatly influenced by the works of *Jean Piaget and Lev Vygotsky*. It is theory of how a learner constructs knowledge from experience, which is unique to each individual. The terms "cognitive constructivism" and "social constructivism"

Table 4.1
Cognitive-Developmental Theory: History of Theory and Research

Premise:	When individuals cooperate on the environment, sociocognitive conflict occurs, thus creating cognitive disequilibrium, which in turn stimulates perspective-taking ability and cognitive development.
Contributors:	Piaget, Vygotsky, Kohlberg, Murray, controversy theorists (Johnsons & Tjosvold), cognitive restructuring theorists
Assumptions:	Focus on what happens within a single person (e.g., disequilibrium, cognitive reorganization)

have become common when talking about this psychological theory. These are two types of constructivism.

4.1 Cognitive Constructivism of Jean Piaget and Cooperative Learning

Cognitive constructivism is based on work of *Jean Piaget*. Piaget's theory has two major parts: "ages and stages", which predicts what children can and cannot understand at different ages, and a theory of development that describes how children develop cognitive abilities. The theory of development is the major foundation of cognitive constructivist approaches to teaching and learning. Piaget's theory of cognitive development suggests that humans cannot be "given" information which they automatically understand and use, they must "construct" their own knowledge. They have to build their knowledge through experience. Experience allows them to create mental images in their head.

In Piaget's theory, individuals are seen as revising their ways of thinking to provide a better fit with reality when faced with discrepancies between their own ways of viewing the world and new information. This the individuals do by making the use of the processes of assimilation, accommodation and equilibration as prescribed by Piaget. According to Piaget, assimilation refers to the ability to explain events based on available cognitive constructions or current schemas. Schemas are referred to the organization of knowledge attained through exploration and adaptation and with changes through the stages of development, becoming more complex as one progresses. Accommodation refers to the ability to change the cognitive construction of schemas to make meaning of surroundings of the natural world. Equilibration is the process of moving back and forth between disequilibrium and equilibrium and where equilibrium refers to a sense of stability or comfort that is achieved through the process of adaptation (assimilation and accommodation) of new information experienced in daily life.

According to *Piaget*, when an individual comes under the influence of social interaction, it incites a cognitive conflict within the individual which results in efforts to reestablish equilibrium. Individuals have their own unique schemas of knowledge or events they have interpreted based on their own ability of cognitive construction. For developing further, individuals require dissatisfaction with one's current understanding of a problem or a change in perspective. This is possible only through social interaction when during interaction cognitive conflict occurs between peers who have different answers to the same question. Social interaction then contributes to directing the individual to accept another view through presentation of the alternatives and consideration of the merits of each. Social influence fosters change through the induction of cognitive conflict and the logical operations carried out by individuals attempting to reconcile their differing views to achieve equilibrium of understanding.

Piaget thus, emphasized cooperation as the ideal form of social interaction promoting development because he believed that the social relations involved in cooperation are the same as the logical relations the children construct in regard to the physical world.

Piaget laid out three conditions under which equilibrium can be achieved in intellectual exchange. The first is that the partners should have a common scale of intellectual values, language and a system of ideas so that they can translate the differing conceptions to common terms. The second condition is that the partners recognize a conservation point where they can justify their difference in point of views and try to reach on agreement on propositions. The third condition is that there should be reciprocity or such mutual understanding between partners that they treat propositions of each, interchangeably. Piaget emphasized cognitive conflict as the working out of differences of opinion by coming to understand the other's perspective and by logically comparing the value of the two perspectives.

The essential elements of cooperative learning viz. face-to-face promotive interaction and interpersonal and small group skills can be said to have been derived on the basis of Piaget's views. Face-to-face promotive interaction and use of interpersonal and small group skills are not only important but essential for solving cognitive conflicts occurring within the cooperative learning groups so that individuals can maximize their own as well as each other's learning.

4.2 Social Constructivism of Lev Vygotsky and Cooperative Learning

Social constructivism is a theory developed by psychologist *Lev Vygotsky*. Vygotsky's theory is very similar to Piaget's assumptions about how children learn, but Vygotsky placed more emphasis on the social context of learning. It stressed the fundamental role of social interaction in the development of cognition as Vygotsky strongly believed that community plays a central role in the process of "making meaning". Unlike Piaget's notion that children development must necessarily precede their learning, Vygotsky argued that learning is a necessary and universal aspect of the process of developing culturally organized, specifically human psychological function. In other words, social learning tends to precede development. Vygotsky contended that learning and development are intertwined from the first day of life and learning cannot be matched to stages but must be determined by assessment of two developmental levels-

(a) Actual developmental level and

(b) The zone of proximal development

The Zone of Proximal Development (ZPD) is the "space" where a MKO (More Knowledgeable Other) viz. teachers, parents and peers may influence the individual's development.

The MKO

The More Knowledgeable Other is somewhat self-explanatory. It refers to someone who has a better understanding or a higher ability level than the learner, with respect to a particular task, process or concept. Although the implication is that the MKO is a teacher or an older adult, this is not necessarily the case. Many times, a child's peer or an adult's children may be the individuals with more knowledge or experience. In fact, the MKO need not be a person at all. Nowadays, electronic tutors are also being used in educational settings to facilitate and guide students through the learning process. The key to MKOs is that they should have (or be programmed with) more knowledge about the topic being learned than the learner does.

The ZPD

The concept of More Knowledgeable Other is integrally related to the second important principle of Vygotsky's work, the Zone of Proximal Development. Taken together, the MKO and ZPD form the basis of the scaffolding component of the cognitive apprenticeship model of instruction. *Vygotsky* defined the ZPD as the distance between the actual development level as determined through problem solving under adult guidance or in collaboration with more capable peers. He believed that when a student is at the ZPD for a particular task, providing the appropriate assistance (scaffolding) gives the student enough of a "boost" to achieve the task. Once, the student, with the benefit of scaffolding masters the task, the scaffolding can then be removed and the student would then be able to complete the task again on his own.

Vygotsky's model for the mechanism through which social interaction facilitates cognitive development resembles apprenticeship, just like fresh medical graduates are required to carry out their apprenticeship under their seniors, in which a novice works closely with an expert in joint problem solving in the zone of proximal development. The novice is thereby able to participate in skills beyond those that he or she is independently capable of handling. Development builds on the internalization by the novice of the shared cognitive processes, appropriating what was carried out in collaboration to extend the existing knowledge and skills. Thus, according to *Vygotsky*, the true direction of the development of thinking is not from the individual to the socialized, but from the social to the individual and in this language as a tool plays a significant role.

In Cooperative Learning, when heterogeneous groups are formed on the basis of ability, for example low achievers are placed along with high achievers in the same group, the notion of ZPD and MKO comes into being.

Although both the theories and the research deriving from them emphasize cooperation in cognitive activity, they differ in the extent to which the process of cognitive development is seen as occurring in the cooperative interaction. The theories of *Piaget* and *Vygotsky* basically differ in the mechanisms proposed to underlie social influence, the phase of childhood seen as being open to social influence and the ideal partner and role relations. For Piaget, the cooperation provides information for the individual to use in becoming aware of differing perspectives and in resolving the differences between them. In the Vygotskian perspective, in contrast, the individual makes use of the joint decision making processes itself to expand understanding and skill. Both theories emphasize the importance of a common frame of reference, or intersubjectivity in social interaction but since Vygotsky provides central position to social and Piaget to the individual they differ in the locus of intersubjectivity. In Vygotsky's perspective joint problem solving occurs between partners with guidance by a person who is more skilled, whereas in Piaget's view, individuals work with independence and equality on each other's ideas to solve cognitive conflicts. In Piaget's theory, collaborative problem solving is explained by deriving both cognitive and social processes from the same central intrapsychological process, whereas in Vygotsky's theory, the correspondence between cognitive and social processes is due to the derivation of individual cognitive processes from joint cognitive processes in social contexts. For Piaget, development moves from the individual to the social, and for Vygotsky, development moves from the social to the individual.

Both the theories also differ regarding the right age for the social interaction to be effective. According to Piaget, the young child is largely impervious to social influence because egocentricity blocks the reciprocity and cooperation in considering different points of view. Thus, it is not until middle childhood that children benefit intellectually from social interaction, when logical argument between children with varying points of view becomes possible. Young children would generally find it difficult to consider the logic of another's point of view that they would either continue to see things from their own perspective or switch to the other person's perspective without understanding the rationale and hence without actually advancing developmentally. With egocentrism the three conditions he set for the achievement of equilibrium are not possible. Piaget specified that at the stage of concrete operations (from about 7 to 11 or 12 years), children become able to cooperate and to coordinate points of view. The importance of social interaction and the role of society become still more obvious in the next stage, formal operations, which begin after 11 -12 years. Vygotsky's approach contrasts with Piaget's in its assumption that from the beginning the child is a social being, involved in social exchanges that guide the development of higher cognitive processes. Vygotsky assumed that social guidance aids children in learning to communicate and to plan and remember deliberately from the first years of life. This guidance provides children with the opportunity to participate beyond their own abilities and to internalize activities practiced socially, thus advancing their capabilities for independently managing problem solving. Vygotsky argued that rather than deriving explanations of psychological activity from the individual's characteristics plus secondary social influences, the unit of analysis should be social activity, in which individual functioning develops. Piaget's approach was the reverse-to focus on the individual as the unit of analysis, with social influence overlaid on the individual's activity, after the child becomes able to take another person's perspective. These differences in the timing and centrality of social influence relate to Vygotsky's focus on development of understanding and skills in using cultural tools and Piaget's focus on qualitative shifts in perspective.

The two theorists also attributed varying degrees of importance to the roles of adults and peers. Piaget emphasized peer interaction between companions of equal status. Piaget felt that children's discussions with adults are unlikely to promote cognitive development because of the unequal power relations between adults and children, provided the possibility that adults may be able to interact with children in a cooperative fashion that permits the sort of reciprocity required for children to advance to a new level of equilibrium. For Vygotsky, ideal partners are not equal, but the inequality is in skills and understanding rather than in power. For this reason, interaction with either adults or peers can bring about cognitive growth. But for cognitive development to occur in the course of interacting with a peer, the partner should be 'more capable'.

Thus, we see that in whatever extent the theories of *Jean Piaget* and *Lev Vygotsky* differ in the process of cognitive development occurring in the cooperative interaction, both of them equally emphasize cooperation in cognitive activity. Cooperative learning equally owes its growth on the seeds of both the theories and equally reaps the benefits implicated by them.

5

Cooperative Learning and Behavioural Learning Approach

The behavioural-social perspective presupposes that cooperative efforts are fueled by extrinsic motivation to achieve group rewards (academic and/or nonacademic).

Table 5.1
Behavioural Learning Theory: History of Theory and Research

Premise:	Actions followed by extrinsic rewards (group contingencies) are repeated.
Contributors:	Skinner (group contingencies); Bandura (imitation); Homans, Thibaut & Kelley (balance of rewards and costs); Mesch-Lew-Nevin (specific application to cooperative learning)
Assumptions:	Cooperative efforts are powered by extrinsic motivation to achieve group rewards.

Albert Bandura and *B.F. Skinner* are the main contributors of the behavioural approach of theoretical basis of Cooperative Learning.

5.1 SOCIAL LEARNING THEORY OF BANDURA AND COOPERATIVE LEARNING

Albert Bandura was a prominent social learning theorist who propagated that observation of other's behaviour plays a leading role in learning and acquiring various things concerning one's environment. He put forth the view that individuals do not blindly respond to environmental stimuli. Rather, they pick and choose from many environmental options, basing their decisions on their own insights and past experiences. This they do through vicarious or observational learning, by incorporating and imitating the behaviour of those around. The theory emphasizes that most of what one learns is acquired through simply watching and listening to other people. The children from the very beginning keenly observe the behaviour of others, most commonly of the people nearest to them like parents, members of the family, teachers, the older members of the society, etc. in turn, they try to imitate and do what they observe. Direct experiences no doubt constitute the most effective and powerful sources of one's learning but the role of indirect experiences leading to observational learning can also not be underestimated. In many cases, they prove more desirable, less expensive and more beneficial than the direct experiences. Observational learning provides extra dimensions and opportunities for the learners in addition to their learning through self-experience and direct involvement with environmental consequences. It certainly reduces the need of an individual to go through every experience himself and thus, helps him to learn from the examples of others. An individual first attends to and perceives the behaviour of another individual and then remembers his behaviour in his memory in the form of mental images. Then the observed and remembered behaviour is analyzed by the learner in terms of its acceptability with reference to the demands of his self and his environment and then transformed into action. Finally the behaviour imitated by the learner is reinforced for proper adoption and further continuance. The individual's behaviour is affected by satisfaction and pleasure. In this way, through social learning i.e. learning through observation and modeling an individual learns many things concerning one's behaviour. How one displays love and anger, shows sympathy and prejudices, speaks and writes, dresses and eats, takes initiative or shies away, all depend upon what has been observed, remembered, imitated and reinforced in context of the vicarious or model learning .

Cooperative learning is also synonymous with social learning. It propounds that what individuals learn together today they can apply it individually tomorrow. When individuals work in groups there is maximum social interaction. They keenly observe each others habits, values, attitudes, personality, behaviour, mental thinking processes, etc. and are influenced by these and readily adapt them. Weaker students observe the thinking process and problem solving techniques of brighter students in cooperative groups, remember them and then later on try to put it into action as and when needed. Similarly social skills are learnt by interacting with each other, observing and imitating the best possible styles. When individuals are able to achieve the level desired by them they feel pleasure and satisfaction in learning. In this way, the individuals through social learning not only benefit academically but also socially and psychologically.

5.2 LEARNING THEORY OF B.F. SKINNER AND COOPERATIVE LEARNING

The theory of *B.F. Skinner* is based upon the idea that learning is a function of change in overt behaviour. When a particular Stimulus-Response (S-R) pattern is reinforced (rewarded), the individual is conditioned to respond. Reinforcement is the key element in Skinner's theory. A reinforcer is anything that strengths the desired response. It could be verbal praise, a good grade or a feeling of increased accomplishment or satisfaction. *Skinner* explained drive (motivation) in terms of deprivation and reinforcement schedules. He gave the principles that-

- Behaviour that is positively reinforced will reoccur; intermittent reinforcement is particularly effective ,
- Information should be presented in small amounts so that responses can be reinforced ('shaping'),
- Reinforcements will generalize across similar stimuli ('stimulus generalization') producing secondary conditioning.

Considering the implications of reinforcement theory, it is emphasized that- practice should take the form of question (stimulus)- answer (response) frames which expose the students to the subject in gradual steps, it is required that learner should compulsorily make a response and receive immediate feedback for it and it should be ensured that good performance in the lesson is paired with secondary reinforcer such as verbal praise, prizes and good grades.

In a traditional classroom which is a teacher-fronted classroom, reinforcement for positive learning behaviours usually comes only from the teacher. Indeed, in the typical teacher-fronted classroom, students often feel negatively interdependent with one another, competing against each other for reinforcement from the teacher in such forms as praise and grades. In contrast, in cooperative learning when learners feel positively interdependent toward their peers, they become an alternative source of positive reinforcement for learning.

Working cooperatively they learn the material by questioning each other, explaining each other, remembering and recalling turn by turn and during the process supporting each other by providing feedbacks and reinforcement. This reinforcement encourages students to work hard to succeed and help their group mates succeed at learning tasks, and the use of thinking skills facilitates success in almost any task.

Slavin (1990) and his colleagues have done a great deal of work on cooperative learning from this tradition, developing techniques such as student teams achievement divisions (STAD).

6

Methods/Strategies of Cooperative Learning and Their Implementation

Though there are a number of methods of cooperative learning, the following have received the most attention-

Method / Strategy	*Researcher-Developer*
Complex Instruction	Cohen
Constructive Controversy	Johnson & Johnson
Cooperative Integrated Reading and Composition	Stevens, Slavin & Associates
Cooperative Learning Structures	Kagan
Group Investigation	Sharan & Sharan
Jigsaw	Aronson & Associates
Learning Together	Johnson & Johnson
Student Teams Achievement Divisions	Slavin
Teams-Games-Tournament	DeVries & Edwards
Team Assisted Individualization	Slavin & Associates

These methods/strategies of cooperative learning have been described as under-

1. COMPLEX INSTRUCTION

Complex Instruction is a cooperative learning method based on inquiry and investigation. It was developed by ***Elizabeth Cohen*** in 1986. The most widely used form of this approach is a program called Finding Out/Descubrimiento, a discovery oriented elementary school program developed by Edward DeAvila and Elizabeth Cohen. This method used particularly in bilingual classes, involves students in small group, hands-on science activities directed toward discovery of important scientific principles. Students may work together on experiments to derive principles of magnetism, sound, light, and so on. Materials for Finding Out/Descubrimiento are available in English and Spanish, so that monolingual and bilingual students can work together cooperatively. In addition to learning science, students in Finding Out/Descubrimiento apply mathematics skills in real-life situations and engage in focused discussions that develop English skills for limited-English-speaking children.

Complex Instruction can be considered as an appropriate and promising instructional strategy for academically and linguistically diverse classrooms. When students are involved in learning through Complex Instruction, they interact and use one another as resources. Those who do not read or speak the language of instruction may get help from their peers. They have greater access to understanding than they might during traditional teacher-directed instruction. Peer interaction increases interest and engagement in the task and provides a strong potential for learning. But in academically and linguistically heterogeneous classroom, teachers should safe guard their students from the status problems that may prop up. Status problems are the result of differing expectations for competence: low expectations for low-status students and high expectations for high-status students. These expectations for competence are held by teachers, by classmates, and by the students themselves. Students who lack traditional academic skills or proficiency in the language of the instruction or who are social isolates are too often perceived as low status students. When low status students are in groups, they barely participate, are often ignored and frequently are not given a share of the materials or a turn at the activity. When this occurs, a status problem is recognized. This can lead to learning problems wherein high-status students interact more in the classroom and hence, learn more and low-status students interact less and consequently learn less.

To overcome this problem where the rich get richer while the poor get poorer, Complex Instruction offers two strategies to treat status problems in the classrooms-

The multiple abilities status treatment and Assigning competence to low-status students.

The multiple-abilities status treatment- The multiple abilities status treatment is based on the premise which suggests that intelligence is multi-dimensional (*Gardner*, 1983; *Stenberg*, 1985). So rather than assuming that all students can be ranked along a single dimension of ability, different kinds of intellectual ability are considered. For example, a highly verbal student may have difficulty with tasks that require spatial and visual ability. Likewise, a student poor on vocabulary tests may be a good scientific observer.

In Complex Instruction, the multiple-abilities treatment is provided by the teacher during orientation to the day's work in groups. The teacher may start by naming the different skills and abilities necessary for successful completion of an activity such as diagramming, mathematical concepts, expressing an idea as a cartoon, or creating a three-dimensional model. Such tasks call for abilities such as hypothesizing, estimating, analyzing problems logically, figuring out how something works mechanically or translating a musical or visual message into words. Such activities create a mixed set of expectations for each student approaching the task as the student realize that no one in the group will have all the abilities necessary to do the task but everyone will have some of the abilities. Herein lays the premise of Complex Instruction: Each individual brings valuable and different abilities to the task. All are needed to succeed. The message is not a simplistic "Cooperate because it is nice thing to do" rather, it is "Cooperate because you need each other".

Assigning Competence to low-status students- Assigning competence to low-status students has even stronger potential to boost up their participation and performance in group activity. Assigning competence is a positive evaluation done by the teacher. It is a public statement that specifically recognizes the intellectual contribution different students make to the group work task. Assigning competence to students especially low-status students by the teacher must be public, so that the student's classmates hear it, it must be specific so that the student and the group know exactly what he or she did well and also it must make the intellectual ability demonstrated by the student relevant to the work of the group. This can be done by the teacher on the spot during group work or later during wrap-up or orientation the next day. This changes the expectations students hold for themselves and each other. The teacher when demonstrates to the students that they each have intellectual abilities that are highly esteemed in society, such as planning, organizing, creating, performing, reasoning or inventing it not only raises one student's self esteem, but also raises the groups expectations for that student. Public recognition by the teacher creates a dais where the group is more likely to be directed to talk to that student, which in turn increases interaction. When low-status students have access to the interaction, they also have greater access to learning.

In Complex Instruction, treatment of status problems takes place in the context of a transformed classroom, there is a special management system and the curricular materials are designed to enable students to excel using multiple intellectual abilities.

In Complex Instruction, the class is divided into groups of four to five students, each group working in a different task simultaneously. As in Complex Instruction, tasks are uncertain and open-ended; it becomes delegate authority to the students so that interaction amongst them is maximized. Delegation of authority to students is done through-

- Use of an activity card with instructions for the task and individual reports to be completed by each member of the group.
- The development of a set of cooperative norms guiding student behaviour and
- A set of procedural roles that helps the group get its work done.

The Activity Card and Individual Report- The teacher transforms his/her authority to the students and assigns tasks through written instructions on an activity card. Instructions can be written in any language used in the classroom or can include visuals that depict the tasks for those students who have difficulty reading. Through the activity card, the students are made to work on their own, to decide what and how to do their work. This promotes positive interdependence and promotive interaction between them. To ensure individual accountability at the same time, students are required to complete an individual report at their learning stations.

Developing Cooperative Norms- As with other models of Cooperative learning, Complex Instruction stresses preparation of students for the new behaviours needed for working in small groups. The two central norms that Complex Instruction uses as basic rules of the classroom are-

"You have the right to ask anyone else in your group for assistance' and

"You have the duty to assist anyone in your group who asks for help".

If students come to feel that they ought to behave in these new ways, they will teach, reinforce and enforce cooperative behaviours with their peers and this directs their behaviour towards desirable ends.

Procedural/Student Roles- Delegation of authority is supported by giving each student a procedural role to play. The roles which are most widely used are that of a facilitator, materials manager, recorder/reporter, safety officer and harmonizer. The roles selected depend on the age of the students and the nature of the task. The roles are designed to encourage interaction and discussion and to take care of the business of the group.

ROLE OF THE TEACHER

In Complex instruction classrooms, promoting equal access to information and fostering higher order thinking is paramount. So one of the major tasks of the teacher is to encourage and stimulate student interaction through intrinsically interesting, engaging and rich tasks that require students to exchange ideas and materials. This requires specialized curricula.

The role of the teacher when creating curricula for group work or when adapting existing materials to follow the Complex Instruction model is firstly to organize activities around a central concept or "big idea" so that students encounter the concept or idea in different contexts and have multiple opportunities to grapple with the material. Secondly, to keep the activities or learning tasks open-ended or uncertain in their solution as well as in the process by which students arrive at the solution. Open-ended and inherently uncertain tasks increase the need for interaction since students draw upon each other's expertise and repertoire of problem-solving strategies which are rich and varied. Thirdly, a necessary condition for Complex Instruction is to mould or transform the activities into multiple-abilities tasks for successful status treatments.

Overall it takes considerable time to develop expertise in Complex Instruction as a teacher's conceptual understanding of the theory and principles underlying Complex Instruction is related to the quality of implementation in the classroom. Teachers who understand why they are delegating authority to the groups or how status problems come to affect interaction and learning are able to solve problems and adapt instructional strategies to meet the needs of their students. Preparation for employing Complex Instruction involves participation in a yearlong programme that provides teachers with the theoretical understanding and practical experience necessary to maintain high quality implementation. Teachers and administrators must collaborate to support successful implementation of Complex Instruction as restructuring the classroom demands school-level support. The implementation of multiple-abilities curricula requires resources beyond the classroom. It is unlikely that an isolated teacher will be able to collect and organize the materials alone. An instructional assistant, a resource teacher or a team of teachers needs to be given time to work on the task. When implementing Complex Instruction, teachers, like their students benefit when they talk and work together. Teachers who implement Complex Instruction should collaborate at three different levels: within their subject areas, at the grade level and in school wide teams. Successful principals also need to motivate teachers to implement Complex Instruction. With sufficient staff development and school-level support, the Complex Instruction can realize its goals.

2. CONSTRUCTIVE CONTROVERSY

This method was developed by ***David W. Johnson*** and ***Roger T. Johnson***. Within cooperative learning groups, intellectual conflict should be encouraged and nurtured, rather than suppressed or avoided. Educators must understand what controversy is, how students benefit from it, how intellectual conflicts create academic benefits, what the key elements are that make controversy work, and the teacher's role in structuring and managing academic controversies (*Johnson*, 1970, 1979; *Johnson* and *Johnson*, 1979, 1987, 1989; *Johnson, Johnson* and *Smith*, 1986).

Controversy exists when one student's ideas, information, conclusions, theories, and opinions are incompatible with those of another, and the two seek to reach an agreement. For example, if one student says that the answer to a mathematics problem is eleven and another student says that the answer is fourteen, conflicts are possible and the two students must agree on the answer to the problem. Such intellectual conflicts are not only inevitable; they are highly desirable as the absence of conflict within an intellectual endeavor may indicate apathy towards the task and each other. Such conflicts can be managed constructively within a cooperative context. Controversies or conflicts are resolved by engaging in deliberate discourse aimed at synthesizing novel solutions. When controversies are structured within a cooperative learning context, participants are required to research and prepare a position; rehearse orally the relevant information; advocate a position; teach their knowledge to peers; analyze, critically evaluate, and rebut information; reason both deductively and inductively; take the perspectives of others; and synthesize and integrate information into factual and judgmental conclusions that are summarized into a joint position to which all sides can agree. Structured academic controversies are most often contrasted with individualistic learning, debate and concurrence seeking, although they stand out from each other in several ways. In individualistic learning situations there is neither interdependence nor intellectual conflict. In debate, a judge is appointed and students then debate the different positions with the expectation that the judge will determine who presented the better position. It has positive resource interdependence, negative goal interdependence and conflict. In concurrence seeking, students can inhibit discussions to avoid any disagreement and compromise quickly to reach a consensus. Within concurrence seeking there is only positive goal interdependence. Structured academic controversy differs from these instructional methods in having both positive goal and positive resource interdependence as well as by conflict.

A key to the effectiveness of conflict procedures for promoting learning is the mixture of cooperative and competitive elements within the procedure. The greater the cooperative elements and the lesser the competitive elements, the more constructive the conflict. Academic controversies create numerous benefits for students when they occur within cooperative learning groups and are carefully structured to ensure that students manage them constructively.

When students interact, conflicts among their ideas, conclusions, theories, information, perspectives, opinions and preferences are inevitable. Teachers who capitalize on these differences find that academic conflicts can yield highly constructive dividends. Students who participate in academic

Table 6.1
Nature of Instructional Methods

	Controversy	*Debate*	*Concurrence Seeking*	*Individualistic*
Positive Goal Interdependence	Yes	No	Yes	No
Positive Resource Interdependence	Yes	Yes	No	No
Negative Goal Interdependence	No	Yes	No	No
Conflict	Yes	Yes	No	No

controversy recall more correct information, are better able to transfer learning to new situations, use more complex and higher level reasoning strategies in recalling and transferring information learned, and are better able to generalize the principles they learned to a wider variety of situations.

If students are to become citizens capable of making reasoned judgments about the complex problems facing the society, they must learn to use the higher level reasoning and critical thinking processes involved in effective problem solving. To do so, students must enter empathetically into the arguments of both sides of the issue; ensure that the strongest possible case is made for each thought. Participating in structured controversy teaches students of all ages how to find high-quality solutions to complex problems.

Academic controversy also tends to result in more creative insights into the issues being discussed. It increases the number of ideas, the quality of ideas, the creation of original ideas, the use of wider range of ideas, originality, the use of more varied strategies and the number of creative synthesis combining both perspectives.

Being able to manage disagreements and conflicts constructively enables individuals to cope with the stresses involved in interacting with a variety of other people. This results in higher academic self-esteem and greater perspective-taking accuracy.

The hypothesis that intellectual challenge promotes higher-level reasoning, critical thinking, and metacognitive thought is derived from a number of premises:

1. When individuals are presented with a problem or decision, they have an initial conclusion based on categorizing and organizing incomplete information, their limited experiences and their specific perspective.

2. When individuals present their conclusion and its rationale to others, they engage in cognitive rehearsal, deepen their understanding of their position, and discover higher-level reasoning strategies.

3. When individuals are confronted by other people with different conclusions based on other people's information, experiences, and perspectives, they can become uncertain as to the correctness of their views. A state of conceptual conflict or disequilibrium is aroused.

4. Uncertainty, conceptual conflict, and disequilibrium motivate an active search for more information, new experiences, and a more adequate cognitive perspective and reasoning process in hopes of resolving the uncertainty.

5. By adapting their cognitive perspective and reasoning through understanding and accommodating the perspective and reasoning of others, individuals derive a new, reconceptualized, and reorganized conclusion. Novel solutions and decisions are detected that are, on balance, qualitatively better.

Based on these premises, the process of Constructive / Academic Controversy is conducted in five sequential steps that may typically take five class periods.

STEP-1: Organizing Information and Deriving Conclusions

In order to make high-quality decisions, individuals have to think of the proper alternatives, do a good job of evaluating them and choose the most promising one. Individuals agreeing on one specific perspective are grouped together to form a cooperative learning group. The individuals following a specific perspective can be paired together. During the first class period, each pair develops its position and plans how to present the best case possible to the other pair. Near the end of the period, pairs are encouraged to compare notes with pairs from other groups who represent the same position. During this step, learners organize their current knowledge and experiences, within the framework of their perspective, into a conceptual framework from which they can derive a conclusion. The conceptual frameworks formed, however often lead to inaccurate conclusions because of the limitations of perspective, one's expectations and mental set at the time, a tendency to give one's dominant response to the situation, or fixation on the first seemingly satisfactory solution generated.

STEP-2: Presenting and Advocating Positions

During the second class period, each pair makes its presentation. Each member of the pair has to participate in the presentation. Students present and advocate position to others who, in turn, are advocating opposing positions. Members of the opposing pair are encouraged to take notes and listen carefully. Decisions and conclusions are then reached through a process of argument and counterargument aimed at persuading others to adopt, modify or drop positions.

STEP-3: Being Challenged by Opposing Views

During the third class period, the group members discuss the issue following a set of rules to help them criticize ideas without criticizing people, differentiate the two positions, and assess the degree of evidence and logic supporting each position. Individuals' conclusions are challenged by the advocates of opposing positions. Members critically analyze each other's positions in attempts to discern weaknesses and strengths. They attempt to refute opposing positions while rebutting the attacks on their position. At the same time, they are aware that they need to learn the information being presented and understand the perspective of the other group members.

STEP-4: Conceptual Conflict and Uncertainty

Hearing other alternatives being advocated, having one's position criticized and refuted, and being challenged by information that is incompatible with and does not fit with one's conclusions leads to conceptual conflict and uncertainty. When faced with intellectual opposition within a cooperative context, students ask each other for more information. Conceptual conflict motivates an active search for more information in hopes of resolving the uncertainty. So, during the fourth period, the pairs reverse perspectives and present each other's positions and drop all advocacies, they search for more information, seek to understand opposing positions and rationales and attempt to view the situation from opposing perspectives and begin developing a group report that synthesizes the best evidence and reasoning from both sides.

STEP-5: Reconceptualization, Synthesis, Integration

The purpose of constructive controversy is to create a synthesis of the best reasoning and conclusions from all the various alternatives. It is the intellectual bringing together of ideas and facts and engaging in inductive reasoning by restating a large amount of information into a conclusion or summary. The dual purpose of synthesis is to arrive at the best possible decision or solution and to find a position that all group members can agree on and commit themselves to. During the fifth period, the report is finalized and prepared by adopting the process of synthesis and integration (the teacher evaluates reports on the quality of the writing, the logical presentation of evidence, and the oral presentation of the report to the class), the group's conclusions are presented to the class (all members of the group are required to participate orally in the presentation), students each take an individual test, and if every member of the group achieves up to criterion, they all receive bonus points, and the group processes how well it worked together and how it could do even better next time.

ROLE OF THE TEACHER

Although controversies can operate in a beneficial way, they will not do so under all conditions. Whether there are positive or negative consequences depends on the conditions under which controversy occurs and the way in which it is managed. The teacher occupies a major role in structuring and managing the controversy. It is for the teacher to see that the task is structured cooperatively and that there are at least two well-documented positions (e.g. pro and con). The choice of the topic depends on the interests of the teacher and the purpose of the course.

The teacher should prepare the instructional materials so that group members know what position they have been assigned and where they can find supporting information. The materials should have a clear description of the group's task, a description of the phases of the controversy procedure and the interpersonal and small group skills to be used during each phase, a definition of the position to be advocated, with a summary of the key arguments supporting the position and resource materials. Structuring an academic controversy requires a cooperative context, skillful group members and heterogeneity of group members. Heterogeneity among individuals leads to potential controversy and to more diverse interaction patterns and resources for achievement and problem solving. After assigning students to heterogeneous groups of four, the teacher should divide each group into two pairs and assign the pro and con positions to the pairs. Positive interdependence should be structured by highlighting goal interdependence, resource interdependence and reward interdependence. The teacher must also structure individual accountability by ensuring that each student participates in preparing the assigned position, presenting the position, discussing the issue, reversing perspectives, preparing the report, presenting the report and taking an individual test on the material.

No matter how carefully teachers structure controversies, if students do not have the interpersonal and small group skills to manage conflicts constructively, the controversy will not produce its potential effects. So it is the responsibility of the teacher to teach the students the skills of –

- Focusing on the mutual goal of coming to the best possible decision, not winning,
- Conforming others competence while disagreeing with their positions and challenging their reasoning,
- Separating others personal worth from criticism of their ideas,
- Listening to everyone's ideas, even if one does not agree with them,
- First bringing out all the ideas and facts supporting both sides and then trying to put them together in a way that makes sense,
- Taking the opposing perspective in order to understand both sides of the issue,
- Changing one's mind when the evidence clearly indicates that one should,
- Paraphrasing what someone has said if it is not clear,
- Emphasizing rationality in seeking the best possible answer, given the available data and
- Following the golden rule of conflict (act toward your opponents as you would have them act toward you).

At the end of the academic controversy the teacher should help the groups processes how well they worked together and how they could do even better next time.

3. Cooperative Integrated Reading and Composition

Cooperative Integrated Reading and Composition (CIRC) was developed by ***Madden, Slavin*** and ***Stevens*** in 1986. The overall development plan focused on using cooperative learning as a vehicle by which to introduce practices identified in research on reading and writing into routine classroom practice, and to embed cooperative learning within the fabric of the elementary reading and writing program.

The CIRC program consists of three principal elements: basal-related activities, direct instruction in reading comprehension, and integrated language arts/writing. In all of these activities, students work in heterogeneous learning teams.

In basal-related activities, students are assigned to two or three reading groups (eight to fifteen students per group) according to their reading level. After this the students are assigned to pairs within their reading groups and then these pairs are assigned to teams composed of partnerships from two different reading groups. For example, a team might be composed of two students from the top reading group and two from the low group. All the activities within the teams are done in pairs. Students' scores on all quizzes, compositions, and book reports are contributed to form a team score. Teams that meet an average criterion of 90 percent on all activities in a given week are designated "super teams" and receive attractive certificates; those that meet an average criterion of 80-89 percent are designated "great teams" and receive less elaborate certificates. In story related activities, the students are given a series of activities to do in their teams such as- partner reading, story structure and story-related writing, words out loud, word meaning and partner checking. In partner reading, students first read the story silently and then take turns to read the story aloud with their partners alternating after each paragraph. Errors are corrected if any, by the listener when his or her partner reads. In story structure and story related writing, students are given questions related to each narrative story emphasizing the story grammar. In between the story, the students are instructed to stop reading and to identify the characters, the setting and the problem in the story and to predict how the problem will be resolved. At the end of the story, students respond to the story as a whole and write a few paragraphs on a topic related to the story. In the activity words out loud, the students are given a list of new or difficult words used in the story that they must be able to read correctly without hesitating or stumbling. In the word meaning round, the students are given a list of story words that are new in their speaking vocabularies and asked to look them up in a dictionary, paraphrase the definition and write a sentence for each that shows the meaning of the word. After reading the story and discussing it in their reading groups, students also summarize the main points of the story to their partners. They also pretest one another on a list of spelling words each week and then work over the course of the week to help one another master the list. After students complete each of the story related activities, their partners initial a student assignment form indicating that they have completed and or achieved criterion on that task. At the end of three class periods, students are given a comprehension test on the story, are asked to write meaningful sentences for each vocabulary word, and are asked to read the word list aloud to the teacher. Students are not permitted to help one another on these tests. The test scores and evaluations of the story-related writing are major components of students' weekly team scores.

Direct instruction is given to the students one day each week by the teacher in reading comprehension skills such as identifying main ideas, drawing conclusions, and comparing and contrasting ideas.

During integrated language arts writing periods, teachers use a specific language arts/writing curriculum especially developed for the program. Students work on language arts in the same teams as in reading. During three one-hour sessions each week, students participate in a writer's workshop (*Graves*, 1983), writing at their own pace on topics of their choice. Teachers present ten minute mini lessons at the beginning of each period on writing process, style, or mechanics, for example, brainstorming for topics, conducting a peer revision conference, eliminating run-on sentences, or using quotations. Students spend the main part of the period planning, drafting, revising, editing, and publishing their writing. Informal and formal peer and teacher conferences are held during this time. Ten minutes at the end of the hour are reserved for sharing and "celebration" of student writing. Teacher-directed lessons on specific aspects of writing, such as organizing a narrative or a descriptive paragraph, using specific sensory words in a description, and ensuring noun-verb agreement, are conducted during two periods each week, and students practice and master these skills in their teams.

ROLE OF THE TEACHER

One important possibility opened up by the development of CIRC is the use of cooperative learning as the unifying element of school reform. It provides a structure within which it is possible to incorporate identification of story elements, prediction, summarization, direct instruction in reading comprehension and integration of reading and writing within the reading period. To maximize the effectiveness of CIRC, teachers have to efficiently structure the presentation methods for each segment of the lesson. They are required to use a vocabulary-presentation procedure that requires a demonstration of understanding of word meaning by each individual, a review of methods of word attack, oral reading of vocabulary to achieve perfection and use of the meanings of the vocabulary words to help introduce the content of the story. The teachers have to structure story discussions to emphasize such skills as making and supporting predictions about the story and understanding major structural components of the story. Adoption of CIRC by teachers can serve as a basis for fundamental reform of curriculum, instruction and school organization in the elementary grades.

4. GROUP INVESTIGATION

Group Investigation method was developed by ***Yael Sharan*** and ***Shlomo Sharan*** to reduce the dominance of recitation-presentation teaching methods. Group Investigation strives to create a setting responsive to student's questions and productions and offers a variety of ways of increasing active student participation in the learning process. In addition, when students study together in small groups, they help each other and at the same time develop self-direction and responsibility for their learning. The unique character of Group Investigation lies in the integration of four basic features-

(a) Investigation
(b) Interaction
(c) Interpretation and
(d) Intrinsic motivation

Investigation- Group Investigation has its roots in John Dewey's philosophy of education. In Dewey's view, investigation of any subject can incorporate the essential features of the scientific method and thus can educate students in the spirit and method of scientific inquiry. The investigation begins when the teacher poses a challenging, multifaceted problem to the class. In their course of their search for answers to the problem, students construct the knowledge they acquire, rather than having presented to them prepackaged by the teacher. The process of investigation emphasizes student's initiative, as evidenced by the questions they pose, by the sources they find and by the answers they formulate. Students seek out information and ideas in cooperation with their peers and combine it with the opinions, information, ideas, interests and experiences that each one brings to the task. In this way, in a Group Investigation project, the classroom becomes an 'inquiring community' and each student becomes an 'investigator'.

Interaction- Interaction among students is essential to Group Investigation. Contact, talk, mutual assistance and support among students in small groups are part and parcel of the process of Group Investigation. It is the vehicle by which students encourage one another, elaborate on one another's ideas, help each other focus their attention on the task, and even confront one another ideas with opposing points of view. Intellectual and social interactions are the means by which students rework their personal knowledge in light of the new knowledge gathered by the group in the course of the investigation. At each stage of the investigation, students have ample opportunities for interaction. They discuss the plan of their inquiry, they examine a variety of sources and exchange ideas and information, they decide together how to summarize and integrate their findings and they plan how to present their findings to their classmates.

Interpretation- Interpretation is a process of negotiation between each student's personal knowledge and the new knowledge acquired, and between each student and the ideas and information contributed by other members of the group. In Group Investigation, while students conduct their inquiry individually, in pairs and in small groups, they gather a great deal of information from a variety of sources. At regular intervals they meet with other members of their group to exchange ideas and information. Together they attempt to make sense of what their inquiry has yielded. In this context, interpretation is a social-intellectual process par excellence. This process of interpretation through group interaction is consistent with *Dewey's* and *Thelen's* view of education, as well as with the constructivist approach to cognition as developed by Piaget and his followers. Group Investigation provides students with the opportunity to interact with others who have investigated different aspects of the same general topic and who contribute different perspectives on that topic. The cooperative interpretation of information gathered by group members promotes their ability to organize, confirm and consolidate their findings and thus make sense of them.

Intrinsic Motivation- Group Investigation motivates students to take an active role in determining what and how they will learn. It invites them to make individual and joint choices and decisions based on the questions they ask and the problems they seek to investigate. The guidelines they set are the ones they act upon, so that they have a great deal of control over their learning. Also by inviting students to relate the problems they set out to investigate to their own curiosity, experiences and feelings. Group Investigation heightens their personal interest in seeking the information they need. Their investigation draws additional motivating power from their interaction with one another. Group Investigation in particular increases the opportunity to capitalize on the drive and positive interdependence that develops when students study together.

These four features of Group Investigation- investigation, interaction, interpretation and intrinsic motivation are combined in the following six stages of the model-

Stage 1: Class determines subtopics and organizes into research groups. The teacher presents the class with a broad, multifaceted problem often a part of the curriculum that has no single right answer. For a week or two before the onset of the investigation, the teacher displays a variety of resource materials and invites the class to examine them. Books, magazines, stamps, pictures, maps, catalogs, slides, videotapes, and newspapers are some of the materials that may be displayed. Perhaps a lecture on the general problem is delivered, or exploratory discussions during which basic terms are clarified. After the initial exploration, students are ready to formulate and select various questions for inquiry. The teacher writes the general problem on the board and invites students to say what they would like to investigate in order to understand it better. The categories the class determines become the subtopics for separate groups to investigate. Now each student signs up to investigate the subtopic that best reflects his or her interest. Groups are generally formed on the basis of common interest in a specific subtopic.

Stage 2: Groups plan their investigations. Students join their respective research groups and focus their attention on the cooperative planning of the questions they will seek to answer. Group members have three main responsibilities: To choose the questions they will seek to answer, to determine the resources they need and to divide the work and assign roles. Steering committee is also chosen with one member of each group on its board.

Group members discuss their ideas, interests, and views about the scope of their joint inquiry. Cooperative planning at this stage enables each student to choose the method of investigation that best suits him or her. One may prefer to interview people, another may enjoy reading reference material; another may feel most comfortable with visual material. Some students may feel that they learn best when they build something, draw diagrams or see for themselves the actual context of the problem. In the course of their planning discussions, groups take into account their members varied tendencies and preferences and accordingly divide the parts of the investigation among themselves.

Stage 3: Groups carry out their investigations. This stage may last several class periods, each group carries out its plans. Singly or in pairs, group members-Locate information from a variety of sources, Organize and record the data, Report their findings to their group mates, Discuss and analyze their findings. Determine if they need more information and Interpret and integrate their findings. Students are encouraged to locate the information they require from as wide a variety of sources as possible: textbooks, experiments, reference books, pamphlets, magazines, maps, stamps, films, videotapes and other materials and also visit sites such as museums, historical buildings and parks and also consult experts on the subject. The questions that groups decided upon in stage 2 guide them as they locate information. In any one period, a variety of investigating activities can go on simultaneously. Some students may be reading in the classroom or in the school library, others may be conducting an experiment, a few may be summarizing data received from an interview, others may be discussing their interpretation of some interim findings while the teacher meets yet another group. Sometimes during these discussions students become aware of discrepancies between their respective ways of interpreting material or even between sources. At such times they are required to intensify the examination of their sources and seek ways of solving their dilemma. Ongoing discussion and interpretation often lead to new questions that, in turn, call for investigating different resources, conducting new experiments, interviewing additional experts or locating new information in other ways. As investigators, students are required to constantly coordinate their efforts in order to reach their common goal. Each group member becomes the group's 'expert' on a particular aspect of its subtopic and contributes his or her special knowledge to the group. Students interpret the findings individually as well as by discussing them with other members of their group. Towards the end as the investigation draws to a close, recorders note their group's conclusions.

Stage 4: Groups plan their presentations. Students begin to plan how to teach their classmates the essence of what they have learned. Groups decide which of their findings to share with the class and how to present their findings to the class. The main purpose of the presentation is to show the class what the group considers to be the main idea of its findings. In order to do so, the group members integrate all the parts of their investigation and plan a presentation that will be both instructive and appealing to the rest of the class. Presentations can be made in one of many forms: a model, an exhibit, a dramatic skit, role play, a written report, a slide show, a quiz, or a learning station, just to name a few. In addition, groups prepare handouts that list their resources and present the most salient information they have gathered. During planning of the presentation, groups make sure that the main ideas and conclusions of the inquiry are emphasized, everyone in the group takes an active part in the presentation, set and observe time limits for the duration of the presentation, involve classmates from the 'audience' as much as possible by giving them roles to perform, allow time for questions and that all necessary equipment and materials are available.

Stage 5: Groups make their presentations. Groups make their presentations which generally require two class periods to complete. The class is reconvened as "a group of groups," as each group sheds its specific light on the class's common concern. While one group presents the essence of its findings, the rest are a receptive audience. Each group presents the one aspect of the general problem it knows best and simultaneously learns of other facets of the same problem. Before the presentations begin, the teacher and students collaborate in preparing an evaluation sheet, which the class fills out as the presentations take place. The questions for evaluation help students reflect on the clarity, appeal, and relevance of the presentations. They refer to the content of the presentation as well as to the way it is organized. Also, the student's reactions to the presentations and to the summing-up discussion are part of the evaluation process, which is the final stage of the Group Investigation process.

Stage 6: Teacher and students evaluate their projects. Teacher and students evaluate their projects. Evaluation of Group Investigation focuses on the knowledge acquired in the course of the project, as well as on the individual and group experience of investigating. This is done through individual and group tests employing different methods. Students may be asked to demonstrate their ability to draw conclusions from their inquiry and to apply their newly acquired knowledge to related problems and situations. Specific questions that assess these skills may be part of the test that individuals take. They may also be less formally evaluated by a class assignment that integrates the various parts of the investigation project. For example, the class may publish a newspaper that includes all the group summaries as well as new material written specifically for the newspaper. An editorial board made up of a representative of each group, together with the teacher, evaluates the material. Another such assignment is an essay, which calls for individual students to demonstrate what they learned about the general problem and to reflect on the personal significance of their learning. The learning process in stage 6 sustains the skills students employed in all previous stages. They continue to make decisions about their learning; they compare, analyze, explain, and interpret ideas and information.

Role of The Teacher

Incorporating cooperative learning methods in their instructional repertoire requires teachers to change their traditional roles as transmitters of information. As they become more confident in the role of guiding and facilitating cooperative learning, teachers should adopt more diverse and complex cooperative procedures. Group Investigation should be introduced by the teachers when they feel that their students have become used to working together to achieve academic goals. Investigating in group calls for students to use all the interpersonal and study skills acquired in other cooperative learning methods and to apply them to the planning of specific learning goals and also in planning how to integrate and present their findings and together with the teacher collaborate in evaluating their academic and interpersonal efforts. The teacher should pose a challenging, multifaceted problem to the class and which has no single right answer. It should be a part of the curriculum and be relevant to the student's lives in and out of the school. During the first stage of Group Investigation, the role of the teacher is to lead exploratory discussions, provide initial materials, facilitate awareness of interest in problem and coordinate organization of and choosing of subtopic for investigation. The teacher should also circulate among the groups and offer help to those who need it. In stage two when students plan their investigations teacher should help groups formulate realistic plans and help maintain cooperative norms by assigning roles and at the same time help groups locate appropriate resources. For student's convenience, teacher can also prepare a learning station with all the relevant material and have all groups work there in turn. During stage three, when students carry out their investigations and during discussions become aware of discrepancies between their respective ways of interpreting material or even between sources, it is appropriate time for the teacher to help the group out by encouraging them to continue to explore their ideas and perhaps restructure their thinking. When the groups are through the investigations, the teacher should meet the steering committee and hear each group's plan for its report at the end of stage four and make sure that all the group members participate in the presentation. The teacher should post the schedule of presentations so that each group knows when its turn will come. During stage five when groups make their presentations, the teacher should coordinate the presentations, lead discussions of student's comments, establish rules for making comments, lead summing-up discussion and point out connections between subtopics. Although throughout the investigation the teacher has ample opportunities to observe student's academic performance, cooperative behaviours and level of motivation it is imperative for the teacher to evaluate students for understanding of main ideas, evaluate their knowledge of new facts and terms, evaluate integration of all the findings by the group and facilitate student's reflection on process and content of investigation at the last stage. By and large, it is the teacher who initiates the Group Investigation project, determines its duration, and provides most of the resource materials. Hence, advance planning is necessary to carry out this complex role. Throughout the investigation, the teacher should collaborate with the students for emotional involvement, mental stimulation and for the personal significance of the investigation project to make it an authentic learning experience.

5. JIGSAW

The Jigsaw approach was developed as one way to help build a classroom as a community of learners where all students are valued. ***Aronson et al*** in 1978 developed this approach. The basis behind developing this strategy was a passionate desire to reduce the competitive ethos in classrooms that created an artificial reward system under which only some students 'won' and many 'lost'. The process was such designed that made it imperative that the students treat each other as resources. The learning process is so structured that firstly individual competitiveness becomes incompatible with success and secondly success occurs only after students cooperate. In Jigsaw, each group member becomes "specialized" in subject matter and thereby possesses critical information to contribute to classmates. Cooperation and mutual trust become valuable and necessary to academic achievement. Although the Jigsaw approach has been very flexibly applied with limitless variations, there are four generic stages in the process namely,-

Stage 1: Introduction

Stage 2: Focused Exploration

Stage 3: Reporting and Reshaping

Stage 4: Integration and Evaluation

In **Stage 1: Introduction**, the teacher organizes the class into heterogeneous "home" groups, for example:

Home Group "A": Aditya, Seema, Rajesh, Neelu

Home Group "B": Suman, Gopal, Jaya, Amit

The teacher then introduces a topic, text, information, or material to the class and helps the students to understand why they are studying this topic, how it fits with what they have done before, and what they will study in the future. The teacher explains how student learning will be assessed throughout the learning experience. Each member in the home group is given, or selects, a part of the subject matter to be explored.

In **Stage 2: Focused Exploration**, students reorganize to form focus groups. Members of each focus group work together to learn about a specific topic/perspective:

Focus Group 1: Aditya and Suman

Focus Group 2: Seema and Gopal

Focus Group 3: Rajesh and Jaya

Focus Group 4: Neelu and Amit

During this stage, students think out loud in order to clarify their ideas and build understanding together. Sometimes teachers also encourage exploratory writing where students jot down the main ideas they are working on to help them clarify and focus their thinking. Teachers may also provide a guided set of questions to help students explore the ideas in their assigned material.

In **Stage 3: Reporting and Reshaping**, students return to their home groups to take turns describing the ideas generated in their focus groups. During the reporting stage, group members are encouraged to pose questions and discuss ideas in depth. Often as students work through understanding each other's part, they begin to reshape their understanding of the whole.

In **Stage 4: Integrating and Evaluating**, the teacher may design an individual, small-group, or whole-class activity where students can actively integrate their learning. For example, students may carry out a demonstration task in their home groups. The teacher may ask questions to help students reflect on how they worked together and what they might do the same or differently the next time they work together.

The jigsaw activity promotes a natural kind of interdependence through various modifications: the extensive use of pairs, a structured-partner format and the opportunity to revise original thinking after listening to whole class discussion. Students work closely with a partner throughout the activity and also meet with another pair as a group of four a few times to consult. For many students, a pair is a large enough group at the beginning of learning to work together. Alternatively, using pairs can provide a change of pace and often some relief from the challenges of working in fours or fives. Pairs also maximize the access to talking time for all students in the class. Many students experience success in working with just one other person and grow naturally to understand the value of working with others.

Since *Aronson* and his team first published their approach in 1978, several versions have evolved (*Sharan, Hare, Webb* and *Hertz-Lazarowitz*, 1980; *Slavin et al.*, 1985).

Robert Slavin and his colleagues at Johns Hopkins University designated ***Aronson model*** as **Jigsaw I** and created **Jigsaw II** (1986, 1990). This version differs from Aronson's in two fundamental ways: in the outcomes for the process and in the way in which interdependence is structured. The Jigsaw II process requires students to revisit narrative material through the lens of different perspectives to deepen conceptual understanding of significant themes, frameworks, or central ideas.

The second fundamental difference in Slavin's approach is his approach to assessment combined with the use of an extrinsic reward structure. Home groups are established as "teams" comprised of a heterogeneous mix of students by current performance level (high, middle, low). Students teach each other and take individual quizzes that cover all the topics or themes. Individual quiz scores are compiled into a team score. Improvement scoring is used to help low performers' gains make a weighted contribution to the team. Winning teams are highlighted in a newsletter or on a class bulletin board. Thus interdependence is fostered by building a competitive spirit between teams and encouraging cooperation among team members in order to advance the collective team score (*Slavin*, 1990).

Kagan (1990) outlined several variations within the four generic stages of Jigsaw that provide additional support to individual students and strengthen the coaching possibilities in the second stage of the Jigsaw process. *Kagan* also suggested other structures for reconstituted groups.

ROLE OF THE TEACHER

The design of the Jigsaw process ensures that all students in the class are responsible for learning and for teaching what they have learned to others. For some students, this may create an overwhelming sense of pressure to perform when they return to their home group in the third stage of the Jigsaw. Students may worry about their communication skills, learning difficulties or social status, blocking their ability to contribute in their home group. It is then the responsibility of the teacher to support students in different possible ways to counter the potential undue pressure of accountability. To build peer support, the students may be 'twinned' in the home group by the teacher so that two home group members move off together into the focus group and return together to the home group. If the tasks in the focus groups are differentiated so that they require different abilities, the teacher may tailor the task in the focus groups to draw upon the strengths of individual students who may be at risk. Depending on the nature of the task in the focus groups the teacher may design task sheets to help the focus group to organize its work or the teacher may ask the students to jot notes during their focus- group discussion. Notes give students support when they report to the home group. Throughout the Jigsaw process, the teacher may ask students to reflect individually or as a group on how they are working together- both in terms of the academic learning and in terms of how the group is functioning. The periodic pausing directed by the teacher to make sense of what is happening assists students in personal, social and academic development. The teacher may also motivate the students to create a group product. In this way the teacher can recognize both individual contributions and the collective work of the group. Teacher may use a number of ways to assess the learning of students. Teachers can hold conferences with groups and with individual students and also direct students to keep portfolios and use journals to track their own development. For the Jigsaw approach to be a meaningful learning experience, teachers need to make the students believe in the worth of their own contribution and in the worth of the contributions of others. These beliefs develop over time when students are involved in relevant, stimulating, rich activities with many ways of contributing and participating. Students need to become absorbed in open-ended and challenging activities that require them to articulate their thinking, listen to other's ideas, consider new evidence and synthesize and apply information.

6. LEARNING TOGETHER

The Learning Together approach to cooperative learning was developed from the interaction among theory, research, and practice in a five-step process by ***David W. Johnson*** and ***Roger T. Johnson***. First, a review came that synthesized the results of research on cooperative learning to determine the current state of knowledge in the area. Second a series of theoretical models were formulated based on the results of the previous research and the theorizing of Morton Deutsch. Third, Johnson and Johnson conducted a programme of research to validate their theory. Fourth, based on the theory supported by the research, a series of procedures were devised for teachers. Fifth, school districts in many countries were trained to implement cooperative learning. The result of these stages of development showcased the ways cooperative learning may be used in the classroom, highlighted the key elements that make cooperation work, gave a blueprint of the organizational context in which cooperative learning may flourish, defined the process of gaining expertise in using and implementing cooperative learning and also described the expected outcomes from using cooperative learning at the student level and cooperative teams at the school and district levels.

The Learning Together approach to cooperative learning should include all of the following elements:

(a) Three types of cooperative learning procedures used in an integrative way. These three types are formal cooperative learning, informal cooperative learning, and cooperative base groups.

(b) Each cooperative lesson or activity should include the essential components that make cooperation work, namely, positive interdependence, face-to-face promotive interaction, individual accountability, social skills, and group processing.

(c) The repetitive, routine lessons as well as classroom routines should be cooperative (cooperative learning structures).

(d) The organizational structure of schools should be changed from a competitive/individualistic mass-production structure to a cooperative team based structure (the cooperative school).

In Learning Together, the teacher begins the lesson using informal cooperative learning, and then later on formal cooperative learning is used. Students are assigned to the groups and the academic task is also explained to them. Positive goal interdependence is established and positive reward interdependence is also established for example by stating that if the record sheet is accurate, each member will receive 15 points, and if all members of the group achieve 90 percent or better on the test, each member will receive 5 bonus points. Individual accountability is established by the roles assigned and the individual test. While students work in their groups, the teacher monitors them for using interpersonal and small-group skills. At the end of the lesson, the groups hand in their report forms to be evaluated and process how well they worked together by identifying three things members did to help the group achieve and one thing that could be added to improve their group next time. Next, the teacher uses a generic cooperative lesson structure for example to teach vocabulary. Towards the end, the teacher uses informal cooperative learning to provide closure to the lesson by asking students to meet with a person from another group, write out four conclusions they derived from the lesson, and circle the one they believed was the most important. At the end of the school day, the cooperative base groups meet to review what students believe is the most important thing they have learned during the day, what homework has been assigned, and what help each member needs to complete the homework, and to tell each other to have a fun afternoon and evening.

ROLE OF THE TEACHER

The teacher has different roles while organizing cooperative learning activity using all the three types of cooperative learning groups. Teachers should be well aware in the judicious use of the three types of procedures. Teachers should use informal cooperative learning to focus attention on the material to be learned, set a mood conducive to learning, help set expectations as to what will be covered in a class session, ensure that students cognitively process the material being taught and provide closure to an instructional session. While conducting formal cooperative learning teacher should specify the objectives of the lesson both academic and social skill objective to be mastered during the lesson, make a number of pre instructional decisions such as size of the group, the method of assigning students to groups, roles to be assigned to the students, materials needed to conduct the lesson and the arrangement of the room. The teacher should also clearly define the assignment, specify the positive interdependence and individual accountability and provide the criteria for success.

While the students are engaged in learning cooperatively, the teacher should systematically observe and collect data on each group as it works and at the same time intervene to assist students in completing the task effectively and in working together effectively. At the end it is essential to carefully assess student's learning and help the members of the learning groups process how effectively they worked together. Throughout the cooperative learning, teachers may use base groups to improve attendance, to personalize the work required and the school experience and to improve the quality and quantity of learning. All through the teachers should use cooperative learning structures which are standard cooperative procedures for conducting generic, repetitive lessons and managing classroom routines. A competent teacher should have the ability to structure cooperative learning situations automatically without conscious thought or planning. Mastering the use of formal and informal cooperative learning procedures, routine cooperative structures and of cooperative base groups requires an understanding of and ability to implement the components essential for a cooperative effort. Hence, teachers should master the essential elements of cooperation for at least two reasons. First, teachers need to tailor cooperative learning to their unique instructional needs, circumstances, curricula, subject areas and students. Second, teachers need to diagnose the problems some students may have in working together and intervene to increase the effectiveness of the student learning groups. Teachers should have enough training and practice on the essential elements of cooperation to become educational engineers who can take their existing lessons, curricula and courses and structure them cooperatively.

7. STUDENT TEAMS-ACHIEVEMENT DIVISIONS

Student Teams-Achievement Divisions (STAD) developed by ***Robert Slavin*** is the most extensively researched of all cooperative learning methods. It is also very adaptable—it has been used in mathematics, science, social studies, English, industrial arts, and many other subjects, and at levels from second grade to college.

There are three concepts that are central to all Student Team Learning methods: team rewards, individual accountability, and equal opportunities for success. Teams may earn certificates or other rewards if they achieve above a designated criterion. Individual accountability refers to the fact that the team's success depends on the individual learning of all team members. This focuses the activity of the team members on tutoring one another and making sure that everyone on the team is ready for a quiz or other assessment that students will take without teammate help. Equal opportunity for success means that what students contribute to their teams is based on their improvement over their own past performance. This ensures that high, average and low achievers are equally challenged to do their best and the contributions of all team members will be valued.

In STAD, students are assigned to four-member learning teams that are mixed in performance level, sex, and ethnicity. The teacher presents a lesson, and then students work within their teams to make sure that all team members have mastered the lesson. Finally, all students take individual quizzes on the material, at which time they may not help one another. Students' quiz scores are compared to their own past averages, and points are awarded based on the degree to which students can meet or exceed their own earlier performance. These points are then summed to form team scores, and teams that meet certain criteria may earn certificates or other rewards. The whole cycle of activities, from teacher presentation to team practice to quiz, usually takes three to five class periods. STAD is most appropriate for teaching well-defined objectives, such as mathematical computations and applications, language usage and mechanics, geography and map skills, and science concepts.

The main idea behind STAD is to motivate students to encourage and help each other master skills presented by the teacher. If students want their team to earn team rewards, they must help their teammates to learn the material. They must encourage their teammates to do their best, expressing norms that learning is important, valuable, and fun. Students are allowed to work together after the teacher's lesson, but may not help each other with quizzes, so every student must know the material (individual accountability). Students may work in pairs and compare answers, discuss any discrepancies, and help each other with any roadblocks, they may discuss approaches to solving problems, or they may quiz each other on the content they are studying. They teach their teammates and assess their strengths and weaknesses to help them succeed on the quizzes. Since team scores are based on students' improvement over their own past records (equal opportunities for success), any student can be the team "star" in a given week, either by scoring well above his or her past record or by getting a perfect paper, which always produces a maximum score regardless of students' past averages.

Overall STAD can be considered as a generic method of organizing the classroom rather than a comprehensive method of teaching any particular subject. STAD is made up of five major components:

Class presentations, teams, quizzes, individual improvement scores and team recognition.

Class Presentations: Material in STAD is initially introduced in a class presentation which is most often a lecture-discussion conducted by the teacher but could also include audiovisual presentations as well.

Teams: Teams may be composed of four or five students representing a cross section of the class in academic performance, sex and race or ethnicity. After the teacher presents the material, the team meets to study worksheets or other material. The major function of the team is to prepare its members to do well on the quizzes. The team is the most important feature of STAD. The team not only provides the peer support for academic performance that is important for effects on learning, but also provides the mutual concern and respect that are important for effects on outcomes such as Intergroup relations and self esteem. Hence, at every point emphasis is placed on team members doing their best for the team and on the team doing its best to help its members.

Quizzes: After one to two periods of teacher presentation and one to two periods of team practice, the students take individual quizzes. Students are not permitted to help one another during the quizzes. This makes sure that every student is individually responsible for knowing the material.

Individual Improvement Scores: Each student is given a 'base' score derived from the student's average performance on similar quizzes. Then students earn points for their teams based on how much their quiz scores exceed their base scores. The idea behind the individual improvement scores is to give each student a performance goal that the student can reach, but only if he or she works harder and performs better than in the past. Any student can contribute maximum points to his or her team in this scoring system, but no student can do this without showing definite improvement over past performance.

Team Recognition: Teams earn certificates or other rewards if their average scores exceed a certain criterion. Student's team scores may also be used to determine up to five bonus points toward their grades.

ROLE OF THE TEACHER

The teacher has to specifically design curricular materials for STAD. However it is quite easy to do. For each lesson unit planned for teaching through STAD, a teacher needs to prepare a worksheet, an answer sheet and a quiz for the unit. Before starting with the unit the teacher should decide on the number of teams and on the basis of it make copies of team summary sheets; one for each team. While assigning the students to teams, the teacher should balance the teams so that each team is composed of students whose performance levels range from low to average to high and that the average performance level of all the teams in the class is about equal. For this the teacher may use different common methods known or may devise his/her own method for heterogeneous grouping of students. After assigning all students to teams, the teacher should fill in the names of the students on each team on the team summary sheets. In STAD it is essential to determine initial base score for each student. If a teacher starts with STAD after giving three or more quizzes, he/she can use student's average quiz scores as base scores. Otherwise, student's final grades from the previous year can also be considered as base scores. The teacher should teach the lesson unit for one or two periods and then announce team assignments and have students move their desks together to make team tables and let them study the worksheets in their teams for one or two periods after which the teacher may give the first quiz. The teacher should arouse student curiosity at the start of the lesson unit. The teacher should also frequently assess student comprehension by asking questions and make sure that all students work out the problems or examples or prepare answers to the questions. For testing this, the teacher should call on students at random. The teacher should emphasize to students that they are not finished studying until they are sure their teammates will make 100 percent on the quiz. As soon as possible the teacher should figure individual improvement scores and award certificates or other rewards to high-scoring teams. This makes the connection between doing well and receiving recognition clear to students which increases their motivation to do their best. The teacher should also explain to the students the importance of improvement-point system. The teacher should emphasize that the main purpose of the improvement-point system is to give everyone a minimum score to try to beat and set that minimum score based on past performance so that all students have an equal chance of being successful if they do their best academically. Secondly, the teacher should make students realize that the scores of everyone on their team are important as all members of the team can earn maximum improvement points if they do their best and thirdly that the improvement-point system is fair because everyone is competing only with himself or herself trying to improve his or her performance regardless of what rest of the class does. At the end of the activities, the teacher should use his or her imagination and creativity and vary the rewards and recognize team accomplishments from time to time.

8. TEAMS-GAMES-TOURNAMENT

Teams-Games-Tournaments (TGT) was developed by ***DeVries*** and ***Edwards*** on the same line as STAD. TGT is the same as STAD in every respect but one: instead of quizzes and the individual improvement score system, TGT uses academic tournaments, in which students compete as representatives of their teams with members of other teams who are like them in past academic performance. TGT is very frequently used in combination with STAD, adding an occasional tournament to the usual STAD structure.

The class presentations and team formation are similar to STAD. The games which are played are composed of content-relevant questions designed to test the knowledge student's gain from class presentations and team practice. Games are played at tables of three students, each of whom represents a different team. Games are structured within a tournament which is held usually at the end of a week or a unit. For the first tournament the teacher assigns students to tournament tables- the highest three students in past performance to table 1, the next three to table 2, and so on. This equal competition, like the individual improvement score system in STAD, makes it possible for students of all levels of past performance to contribute maximally to their team scores if they do their best. After the first tournament, students change tables depending on their own performance in the most recent tournament. The winner at each table is "bumped up" to next higher table (for example, from table 6 to 5); the second scorer stays at the same table; and the low scorer is "bumped down". In this way if students have been misassigned at first, they will eventually be moved up or down until they reach their true level of performance. The team recognition is on the same pattern as of STAD.

ROLE OF THE TEACHER

The teacher has to specifically design materials for TGT as for STAD. However it is quite easy to do. For each lesson unit planned for teaching through TGT, a teacher needs to prepare games based on the unit. The games have to be organized keeping in mind the performance level of individuals. The uniqueness of games in each tournament provides variety in the class. The teacher should provide recognition to students for their improvement in performance. At the end of the tournament, the teacher should use his or her imagination and creativity and vary the rewards and recognize team accomplishments from time to time.

9. TEAM ASSISTED INDIVIDUALIZATION

At Johns Hopkins University, ***Robert Slavin*** and his colleagues developed and evaluated cooperative learning programs designed specifically for particular subjects and grade levels. Amongst these, the first comprehensive cooperative learning model they developed and researched was Team Assisted Individualization (TAI)—Mathematics, a program that combines cooperative learning with individualized instruction to meet the needs of diverse classrooms. The justification for developing TAI was that firstly it was hoped that it would provide a means of combining the motivational power and peer assistance of cooperative learning with an individualized instructional programme capable of giving all students materials appropriate to their levels of skill in mathematics and allowing them to proceed through these materials at their own pace and secondly through TAI cooperative learning techniques could be applied to solve many of the problems of individualized instruction.

TAI is primarily designed for grades three through six, but has also been used at higher grade levels (up to the college level) for groups of students not ready for a full algebra course. It is almost always used without aides, volunteers, or other assistance. The principal elements of TAI are as follow-

Teams: Firstly the students are assigned to four- to five-member teams. Each team consists of a mix of high, average, and low achievers, boys and girls, and students of any ethnic groups in the class. Every eight weeks, students are reassigned to new teams.

Placement Test: Students are pre tested at the beginning of the program on mathematics operations. They are placed at the appropriate point in the individualized program based on their performance on the placement test.

Curriculum Materials: Following instruction from the teacher, students work in their teams on self-instructional curriculum materials. The units are in the form of books. Each unit has the following parts:

A guide page that reviews the teacher's lesson, explaining the skill to be mastered and giving a step-by-step method of solving the problems.

Several skill practice pages, each consisting of sixteen problems. Each skill practice page introduces a sub skill that leads to a final mastery of the entire skill.

Two parallel sets of ten items, formative tests A and B.

A unit test of fifteen items.

Answer sheets for the skill practice pages and formative tests (located at the back of student books) and answers for unit tests (located in a separate "monitor book").

Teaching Groups: Every day, the teacher teaches lessons to small groups of students drawn from the heterogeneous teams who are at the same point in the curriculum. Teachers use specific concept lessons provided as part of the programme. The purpose of these sessions is to introduce major concepts to the students. While the teacher works with a teaching group, the other students continue to work in their teams on their self-instructional units.

Team Study Method: Following the placement test, the students are given a starting place in the sequence of mathematics units. They work on their units in their teams, using the following steps:

Students locate their units within their books and read the guide page, asking teammates or the teacher for help if necessary. Then the students begin with the first skill practice page in their unit.

Each student works the first four problems on his or her own skill practice page and then has a teammate check the answers against an answer sheet printed upside down at the back of each student book. If all four are correct, the student may go on to the next skill practice page. If any are incorrect, the student must try the next four problems, and so on, until he or she gets one block of four problems correct. If they run into difficulties at this stage, the students are encouraged to ask for help within their teams before asking the teacher for help.

When a student gets four in a row on the last skill practice page, he or she takes Formative Test A, a ten-item quiz that resembles the last skill practice page. Students work alone on the test until they are finished. A teammate scores the formative test. If the student gets eight or more of the ten problems correct, the teammate signs the student's paper to indicate that the student is certified by the team to take the unit test. If the student does not get eight correct (this is rare), the teacher is called in to respond to any problems the student is having. The teacher diagnoses the student's problem, briefly re teaches the skill, and then may ask the student to work again on certain skill practice items. The student then takes Formative Test B, a second ten-item test comparable in content and difficulty to Formative Test A.

When a student passes Formative Test A or B, he or she takes the test paper to a student monitor from a different team to get the appropriate unit test, The student then completes the unit test, and the monitor scores it. Two different students serve as monitors each day. If the student gets at least twelve items correct (out of fifteen), the monitor posts the score on the student's Team Summary Sheet. Otherwise, the test is given to the teacher, who meets with the student to diagnose and remedy the student's problems. Again, because students have already shown mastery on the skill practice pages and formative tests, it is very rare that they fail a unit test.

Team Scores and Team Recognition: At the end of each week, the teacher computes a team score. This score is based on the average number of units covered by each team member and the accuracy of the unit tests. Criteria are established for team performance. A high criterion is set for a team to be a "super team," a moderate criterion is established for a team to be a "great team," and a minimum criterion is set for a team to be a "good team." The teams meeting the "super team" and "great team" criteria receive attractive certificates.

Facts Tests: Twice each week, the students are given three-minute facts tests for which the students are given fact sheets prior to the test to study at home and prepare for the tests.

Whole Class Units: After every three weeks, the teacher stops the individualized programme and spends a week teaching lessons to the entire class covering such skills as geometry, measurement, sets and problem solving strategies. Students work together as a total team on such units as in Students-Teams-Achievement Division.

ROLE OF THE TEACHER

The teacher's role is significant in assigning students to teams and placing them at the appropriate point in the individualized programme based on their performance on the placement test. Teachers should make extensive use of manipulatives, diagrams and demonstrations so that the students may understand the connection between the mathematics they are doing and familiar real-life problems. The teacher should diagnose immediately and remedy the student's problem if he or she is unable to complete the Formative test A or B successfully. The teacher should re-teach the skill and then ask the student to work again on the skill practice items. As a reward for their performance, attractive certificates prepared by the teacher motivate and encourage students to work harder to meet the established criterion.

10. COOPERATIVE LEARNING STRUCTURES

The structural approach to cooperative learning was developed by ***Spencer Kagan***. The basic premise of the structural approach is that there is a strong relation between what students do and what they learn. That is, interactions in the classroom have a profound effect on the social, cognitive, and academic development of students. The construction and acquisition of knowledge, the development of language and cognition, and the development of social skills are largely a function of the situations in which students interact. For this reason, a major direction of the structural approach has been to quantify classroom interactions and to analyze them in terms of their effects on the students. In this way, teachers can be provided with the means to direct the interaction of students in ways that will result in a range of learning outcomes. It is relatively easy for teachers and students to learn various social interaction sequences, called "structures." Because these structures have different learning outcomes, the teacher who knows and uses a range of structures can efficiently produce specific academic, cognitive, and social outcomes among students. A full mastery in the use of structures includes an understanding and manipulation of the elements of structures, as well as an understanding of how to combine structures to create the sequences of activities we know as lessons. Understanding and use of structures complements other approaches to cooperative learning.

Elements are the most basic unit of classroom behaviour. An element can have three components: actors, actions, and recipients. If we say, the teacher has given a writing assignment and students are writing independently then this is an element. Individual students are actors and writing is action. The element can be given a name- "Individuals Write". In another situation, a teacher instructs the class. Once again, there is an actor (teacher) and an action (instruction), but now there are also recipients (the class). The name of the element reflects all three components: "Teacher Instructs Class."

Kagan and *Kagan* (1992) have developed roughly 200 classroom "structures", such as Timed pair share, Folded value line, Corners, Circle the sage, Team pair solo, Find the Fib, Think Pad Brainstorming, Inside/Outside Circle, Number Heads Together, Stir-the-Class, Rally Robin, Round Robin, Round Table, Talking Chips, Pair Discussion, Team Interview, Pair Interview, Three-step Interview, Think-Pair-Share, Draw a gambit, etc. to name a few which may be thought of as steps to classroom activities. These structures stress positive interpersonal peer relationships, equality, self-esteem, and achievement. Students can work together by following the steps to the structure, using material or content selected by the students themselves or by the teacher.

The structures have various aims, such as: building team spirit and positive relationships among students; information sharing; critical thinking; communication skills; and mastery (learning/remembering) of specified material. Many of the structures can fulfill a number of aims simultaneously, depending on how the teacher uses them. Structures can be mixed and matched, and adapted to the particular student group. Some of the structures developed by Kagan are-

(A) Timed pair share

Student's pair off, then number off, 1- 2. The teacher chooses a number, 1 or 2, to speak first. That student speaks about a specified topic for a specified length of time. The other student listens quietly and can nod or smile, but cannot speak or interrupt the speaker. After the allotted time has elapsed, the other student speaks for the same period of time on the same, or another, stipulated topic, with her or his partner in the listener role. After both partners have had equal opportunity to speak, the teacher randomly chooses a number of students, and asks them to summarize what their partners have said. (In a small class, all students could perhaps report.)

This structure encourages self-expression and idea exchange by having students "share the floor" equally. Listening is encouraged. Students' need to summarize their partner's contribution after the exchange is complete (students cannot accomplish this step without listening). If the teacher does not wish to call on all students to report what has been said, randomly choosing a few students encourages all students to be ready to do so. Students do not know in advance whether or not they will be chosen to report, so they prepare in the event they will be chosen.

(B) Folded value line

A problem, or issue, is raised (e.g., U.S. policy towards Iraq; capital punishment; building shelters for the homeless). The teacher elicits which students are strongly supportive of, or against, the issue or idea via a show of hands. Students who feel strongly for or against the issue stand at either end (the "poles") of the Value Line, where one end of the line represents strong support for an issue/concept, and the other represents its opposite. The rest of the class physically position themselves along the line at the point reflecting their own opinion. Thus, those who feel squarely in the middle of an issue stand at the middle, while those who feel rather strongly in agreement with either "pole" stand near that end of the line.

For students to first think about and articulate views with others holding similar views, students can pair off with persons standing next to them in the line. In pairs, they can exchange opinions and explain rationales for their viewpoints. This can also be done in groups of three or four. It can also be practiced first in pairs, followed by two pairs joining to create a group of four, participating in an idea exchange which includes reiteration of points made during the first pair exchange. Summarizing earlier conversations gives students additional language practice (in language courses) and/or helps students find out what was heard/understood/remembered.

Subsequently, for students to listen to views different from their own, the line can be divided in half. The two halves can then be lined up as two parallel lines of students facing each other. To illustrate, if you have 24 students in a class standing in a single line, with person 1 strongly supporting the issue/statement, and person 24 being strongly against it, the line would initially look like this:

1 2 3 4 5 6 7 8 9 10 11 12 13 14 15 16 17 18 19 20 21 22 23 24

The teacher can then ask students to divide the line between persons 12 and 13. Person 13 leads the second half of the line over to person 1. The second half of the line then thus pairs off with the first half like this:

1 2 3 4 5 6 7 8 9 10 11 12

13 14 15 16 17 18 19 20 21 22 23 24

Students can now exchange opinions easily with the person standing across from them. The lines can be repeatedly divided and refolded to regroup students, who then repeat their idea exchanges, to allow further airing of diverse views. It is also possible to combine this structure with ones like the Timed Pair Share, in which student exchanges are structured for equal participation via time limits and rotating speaking order.

A final step can be for randomly selected students to orally summarize to the class the views they heard, or for students to write a paper for homework that describes the breadth of opinions they heard, complete with supporting and opposing arguments that were given. Students could also be instructed to write/speak from the point of view of an opinion they heard which is opposite, or very unlike, their own opinion, rather than their own, to encourage perspective-taking.

This structure can be used to encourage self-expression, listening, paraphrasing, turn taking, and trying to understand and appreciate various viewpoints. Listening to, and then evaluating, various viewpoints boosts critical thinking skills as students consider an issue from various angles. Students can be asked to note, for example, the strong points of each diverse view, or to come up with a composite view incorporating what they believe to be valuable in all viewpoints.

(C) Corners

As with the previous structure, Corners can be used to have students express, and listen to, various opinions on a topic, honing listening, critical thinking, and self-expression skills. The teacher can make each corner of the classroom represent a stipulated view. For example, three possible corners could constitute For, Against, and Undecided relative to a topic. Students move to the corner that represents their viewpoint. Next, students discuss their opinions, or respond to a comment, within their corners. This could first be done in pairs, and later with pairs joining other pairs to make groups of 4, or with subsequent changes of partners to form new pairs.

Students can begin by summarizing their earlier conversation to their new partner(s). Summarizing or repeating ascertains whether the listener listened and understood, and helps validate the ideas of former speakers. The views of all members in one corner can be aired for the benefit of the entire corner after ideas have initially been exchanged in smaller groups. For example, students stand in a circle in the corner, and each person summarizes what the person on their left said.

Asking students to summarize what another person said encourages them to listen to others, since if they haven't listened, they will not be able to complete this task.

After students have finished their in-corner discussions, they can rotate around to other corners in order to share their corner's viewpoints. One way to do this is for the teacher to randomly select two representatives from each corner to go to another corner and summarize their corner's viewpoint. They can rotate to all other corners, making their presentation to each new corner; these presentations can be performed within specified time limits to give all representatives an equal chance to speak. The final step could include randomly choosing students, other than rotating representatives, to report to the class on what was expressed, heard, or learned.

(D) Team statements; Blackboard share

Students first think about a stipulated topic alone, such as- What can be done to rectify economic disparities? Or what can be done to alleviate gender based job discrimination? After students have had time to think and perhaps take notes if they wish they share their ideas in pairs or small groups.

Next, students again work alone and devise one statement that reflects their view. Students then alternate presenting their individual statements to each other, allowing other students in their group to ask for clarification, or further information. The team then creates a Team Statement that represents an opinion everyone in the group agrees with relative to the topic.

After this, (some or all, depending on class size) groups in the class share their team statements orally, or in writing, with the rest of the class. One simultaneous method of reporting, called Blackboard Share is a structure that can be used at this stage. Blackboard Share requires the teacher to section off portions of the blackboard equally for groups to use. After groups write their Team Statements on the board, these can be viewed/ discussed by the entire class.

If not all teams share (such as in very large classes), one technique is for the teacher to randomly choose only some teams to share. Since no team knows in advance which teams will share, all prepare in the event they are called on to share.

Team Statements is designed to give students practice in self-expression, consolidating views, and reaching a consensus despite differing opinions. Blackboard Share can be used to have students simultaneously summarize any individual or team view or result in writing for the whole class.

(E) Draw a gambit

A "gambit" is a sentence or expression that can be used orally during a face-to-face interaction. "Draw a gambit" can be used to help students learn and practice social skills (in a native or foreign language). In a foreign or second language course, expressions socially acceptable in the target culture could be the focus of instruction.

Students, or the teacher, can create expressions to be used in interactions focusing on a specific skill, such as showing interest in what is being said, disagreeing politely, or praising the speaker. These expressions are then written down on strips of paper by students (for example, after being copied off the blackboard), and placed in a deck or pile. Students, in pairs, or groups, then have a conversation. While listening, listeners draw expressions from the deck and use them during the interaction in ways they think are appropriate. Teachers or peers can monitor this as desired; for example, through real time observation followed by commentary, or responding after listening to or watching audio- or video-taped exchanges.

This structure helps students practice socially acceptable language. The goal is to help create a positive ethic in the class by having students practice skills such as praising (being verbally supportive), or disagreeing politely (avoiding threatening or non-peaceful manners of communication), etc. This instruction can be combined with teaching socially acceptable body language, for example, modeled by the teacher, practiced in groups, and monitored by other learners and the teacher.

(F) Paraphrase passport; Rally robin

Paraphrase Passport requires students engaging in a group discussion to paraphrase what others have said. Before a student can go on to offer their own opinion or input, they must paraphrase what was last said. The person whose statement was paraphrased indicates whether the speaker has correctly captured their meaning. Once the speaker is satisfied that she or he has been accurately paraphrased, the discussion continues with the next speaker's comments. Thus, each person taking a conversational turn must paraphrase the prior speaker's comments before giving their own ideas.

This structure aims to give all speakers in the group a chance to be heard and feel understood. It is also a useful device for checking comprehension in a language class. It can be combined with other structures such as Rally Robin. Rally Robin is a structure requiring students to alternate speaking in a set order. It is used so that all students take turns speaking, so that everyone will receive an equal chance to participate.

(G) Three-Step Interview

Each member of a team chooses another member to be a partner. During the first step individuals interview their partners by asking clarifying questions. During the second step partners reverse the roles. For the final step, members share their partner's response with the team.

This structure can be used for listening, self-expression and paraphrasing.

(H) Round Robin Brainstorming

Class is divided into small groups (4 to 6) with one person appointed as the recorder. A question is posed with many answers and students are given time to think about answers. After the "think time," members of the team share responses with one another round robin style. The recorder writes down the answers of the group members. The person next to the recorder starts and each person in the group in order gives an answer until time is called.

This structure can be used to develop patience for turn taking and listening one another's views without criticizing. It also provides equal chance of expression to each and every member of the group.

(I) Numbered Heads Together

A team of four is established. Each member is given numbers of 1, 2, 3, 4. Questions are asked of the group. Groups work together to answer the question so that all can verbally answer the question. Teacher calls out a number (two) and each two is asked to give the answer.

The structure is used to help and encourage each other in understanding the material.

(J) Team Pair Solo

Students do problems first as a team, then with a partner, and finally on their own. It is designed to motivate students to tackle and succeed at problems which initially are beyond their ability. It is based on a simple notion of mediated learning. Students can do more things with help (mediation) than they can do alone. By allowing them to work on problems they could not do alone, first as a team and then with a partner, they progress to a point they can do alone that which at first they could do only with help.

(K) Circle the Sage

First the teacher polls the class to see which students have a special knowledge to share. For example the teacher may ask who in the class was able to solve a difficult math homework question, who had visited New Delhi, who knows the chemical reactions involved in how salting the streets help dissipate snow. Those students (the sages) stand and spread out in the room. The teacher then has the rest of the classmates each surround a sage, with no two members of the same team going to the same sage. The sage explains what they know while the classmates listen, ask questions, and take notes. All students then return to their teams. Each in turn, explains what they learned. Because each one has gone to a different sage, they compare notes. If there is disagreement, they stand up as a team. Finally, the disagreements are aired and resolved.

ROLE OF THE TEACHER

The teacher creates elements. That is, the teacher chooses a combination of actors, the action, and the recipients most effective to reach a given learning objective. For example, if a teacher's objective were for each student to find out what one other student in the class did over the summer, a single element might be the perfect tool. The teacher could simply ask each student in the class to pair up with another and interview his or her partner. "Individuals Interview Partners" works well to accomplish this objective.

In a cooperative learning classroom with eight teams, if the teacher wanted each student in each team to know what all of his or her fellow teammates did, a single "Individuals Interview Partners" would not work. A single element cannot accomplish the teacher's goal. Each element has its domain of usefulness, and elements are selected according to which would be most appropriate for a desired objective. In this case, where the desired result is beyond the domain of a single element, a combination of elements is used to accomplish the objective. Elements may be combined to form structures. The appropriate structure is chosen according to the objective at hand and their usefulness. The teacher should keep in mind the following considerations when determining the domain of usefulness of a structure:

(a) What kind of cognitive development does it foster?
(b) What kind of social development does it foster?
(c) Where in a lesson plan does it fit?
(d) What kind of curriculum does it deliver?

Structures can be tailor-made by the teacher to meet desired social, cognitive, and academic objectives. Existing structures can be modified to fit the context in which they are being used. Modifying structures is based on understanding elements.

By the flexible combination of elements, the teacher gains the ability to choose the most appropriate structures for desired objectives and the ability to create new structures for objectives that he/she may not envision at the moment.

Although the basic principles of cooperative learning do not change, there are several variations and each of the method has its own implementation procedure. But still some common basic steps involved in the successful implementation of the cooperative learning activities can be identified.

7

Structuring Cooperative Learning in the Classroom

The essential elements of cooperation are positive interdependence, individual and group accountability, face-to-face promotive interaction, interpersonal and small group skills and group processing. Systematically structuring these basic elements into group learning situations helps ensure cooperative efforts and enables the disciplined implementation of cooperative learning for long-term success.

The following steps elaborate in detail the procedure for structuring cooperative learning-

1. SPECIFYING INSTRUCTIONAL OBJECTIVES

Two types of objectives have to be specified before the cooperative lesson begins. These are academic objectives and social skills objectives. The academic objectives need to be specified at the correct level of instruction according to a conceptual or task analysis. The social skills objectives detail out what interpersonal and small group skills are to be emphasized during the lesson.

2. DECIDING THE SIZE OF THE GROUP

Optimal size of the cooperative learning group should range from two to six members per group. A number of factors should be considered in selecting the size of a cooperative learning group. It is better to start with pairs or threesomes. Larger the group, larger the range of abilities, expertise and skills and at the same time larger is the time requirement so that everyone has a chance to speak and also larger requirement of members to be highly skilled. Decision of the size of the group should be based on the materials available or the specific nature of the task. Small groups of two to six members are more effective because they take less time to get organized, they operate faster and there is more 'air time' per member.

3. ASSIGNING STUDENTS TO GROUPS

Students can be assigned to the groups using a random or stratified random procedure to make the group heterogeneous. Student selected groups often tend to be homogenous with high achieving students working with high achieving students, males with males and females with females. Teacher made groups often have the best mix of students because the teachers can put together optimal combination of students. The teacher can use many different ways to assign students to learning groups. For example, the students can be randomly assigned to groups by having them count off and place the "ones" together, the "twos" together and so forth, placing non-task oriented students with task oriented peers, asking students to list two peers with whom they would like to work then, place them in a learning group with one person they chose and one or more students selected by the teacher. Assigning of students to groups can be considered as a creative and manipulative task wherein the teacher uses his/her experience and creativity to keep the eagerness and curiosity of students aroused at all the times. The selection of the duration of the cooperative learning group also rests with the teacher who on the basis of instructional unit takes the decision about the cooperative learning group being formal, informal or base group.

4. ASSIGNING GROUP ROLES

When assigning group roles, one must try to ensure that each group includes students that possess four types of skills- forming skills, functioning skills, formulating skills and fermenting skills. Each group member is assigned a responsibility/role that must be fulfilled for the group to function effectively. These may include a researcher- to get the needed materials for the group, a recorder- to write down the group's proceedings, an encourager-to reinforce member's contributions, an observer-to keep track of how well the group is cooperating. Group roles should be assigned keeping in view the demand of the instructional task. Some tasks may require students to pose as scientists, some as lawyers, and some as judges some as craftsmen and so on. Group roles may be crafted and assigned by the teachers as per the requirement of the task and to maintain a novelty in class.

5. ARRANGING THE ROOM

The room arrangement is very important for lesson development. The furniture of the room should be so adjusted that members of a group are able to sit close enough to communicate clearly and effectively without disrupting the other learning groups and also the teacher should have a clear access lane to every group. Within each learning group, students need to be able to see all relevant task materials and each other, to converse with each other without raising their voices, and to exchange ideas and materials in a comfortable atmosphere. Placing students at a rectangle table where they cannot have eye contact with all the other members does not serve the purpose. Also, the groups need to be far enough apart that they do not interfere with each other's learning.

6. EXPLAINING THE ACADEMIC TASK

Before beginning the task, the teacher should tell the class- what to do to complete the assignment and how to do it. A few steps should be followed in explaining the task such as the assignment should be explained to the students which should be a clear, measurable task. Then to ensure transfer and retention, lesson objectives should be explained which should be stated as outcomes. Next, the teacher should explain the concepts, principles and strategies to be used by the students during the lesson and relate them to students past experience and prior knowledge. The procedures to be followed by the students to complete the assignment should also be explained. This keeps the students on task and helps ensure a responsible behaviour. Lastly, the teacher should ask the students some specific questions to check their understanding of the assignment. Such questioning ensures two-way communication and guarantees that the assignment has been given effectively and that the students are ready to complete it.

7. EXPLAINING CRITERIA FOR SUCCESS

Cooperative learning requires criterion-based evaluation, which means adopting a fixed set of standards and judging the achievement of each student against these standards. Thus, at the beginning of the lesson, teachers should clearly explain the criteria by which the student's work would be evaluated. The criteria for success should be structured so that students may reach it without penalizing other students, and groups may reach it without penalizing other groups. The criteria should be tailored to be challenging and realistic for each individual group member. The teacher may say, "Before the group is not finished, every member must demonstrate mastery". To promote inter-group cooperation, the teacher may say, "If the whole class can score over 80 percent correct on the mathematics test, each student would receive three bonus points."

8. STRUCTURING POSITIVE INTERDEPENDENCE

The following saying by *Alexandre Dumas*, "*We instead of me, all for one and one for all*" clearly explains the meaning of positive interdependence. As, within a football game, the quarterback, who throws the pass and the receiver who catches the pass are positively interdependent, the success of one depends on the success of the other. It takes two to complete a pass. One player cannot succeed without the other. Both have to perform competently to assure their mutual success. If one fails, they both fail.

Similarly, the first requirement for an effectively structured cooperative lesson is that students believe that they "sink or swim together." Within cooperative learning situations, students have two responsibilities:

(a) Learn the assigned material, and

(b) Ensure that all members of the group learn the assigned material.

The technical term for that dual responsibility is positive interdependence. Positive interdependence exists when students perceive that they are linked with group mates in such a way that they cannot succeed unless their group mates do (and vice versa) and/or that they must coordinate their efforts with the efforts of their group mates to complete a task. Positive interdependence promotes a situation in which students:

(a) See that their work benefits group mates and their group mates' work benefits them, and

(b) Work together in small groups to maximize the learning of all members by sharing their resources to provide mutual support and encouragement and to celebrate their joint success.

When positive interdependence is clearly understood, it establishes that:

(a) Each group member's efforts are required and indispensable for group success (i.e., there can be no "free-riders").

(b) Each group member has a unique contribution to make to the joint effort because of his or her resources and/or role and task responsibilities.

Positive interdependence within a learning group can be structured in a number of ways. They are -

(i) **Positive Goal Interdependence**- Students should perceive that they can achieve their learning goals if and only if all the members of their group also attain their goals. The group is united around a common goal — a concrete reason for being. To ensure that students believe they "sink or swim together" and care about how much each other learns, one has to structure a clear group or mutual goal, such as "learn the assigned material and make sure that all members of the group learn the assigned material." By doing so, common purpose is established. Goals as well as objectives can be determined by teachers and students.

(ii) **Positive Reward/ Celebration /Incentive Interdependence**- Each group member is given the same award when the group achieves its goals i.e. a mutual reward is given for successful group work and members efforts to achieve it. Success depends on all team members reaching that goal. To supplement goal interdependence, one can add joint rewards (e.g., if all members of the group score 90% correct or better on the test, each will receive 5 bonus points). Sometimes teachers may give students:

a group grade for the overall production of their group, an individual grade resulting from tests, and bonus points if all members of the group achieve the criterion on tests. Regular celebrations of group efforts and success enhance the quality of cooperation.

(iii) **Positive Resource Interdependence**- Only a portion of the resources, information, or materials necessary for the task to be completed are provided to each group member; the members' resources have to be combined for the group to achieve its goals. Teachers can highlight the cooperative relationships by giving students limited resources that must be shared (pens, scissors and glue, one copy of the problem or task per group) or giving each student part of the required resources that the group must then fit together.

(iv) **Positive Role Interdependence**- Complementary and interconnected roles are assigned to each member. The roles relate to the task and act as a means to help the group function more effectively. By having each group member perform a role, an emphasis is placed on the value of that person to the group. There are two types of roles: working roles (reader, writer, summarizer, time-keeper, etc); social roles (encourager, observer, noise monitor, energizer, etc.).

(v) **Positive Identity Interdependence**- Group members should establish a shared identity which facilitates joint pride. The sense of belonging to a group is strengthened through a name, motto, logo, flag, song, secret handshake, etc. This joint identity can be facilitated by the teacher or can be established by pupils. The outcome is a group that functions more cohesively.

(vi) **Positive Task Interdependence**- Division of labour is created so that the actions of one group member have to be completed if the next member has to complete his/her responsibility. In this way, Overall team task is accomplished by completing a series of sub-tasks in an established step-by-step order. Each group member is held responsible for completing one step in the sequence. Through sequencing, group members feel more interdependent.

(vii) **Positive outside Force Interdependence**- The group is placed in competition with some outside force. Group members work together, striving to beat that outside force (other groups, time, the group's previous score, etc.). Outside force is a means or way to bring pupils together so that they feel interdependent and do their best to win the competition.

(viii) **Positive Fantasy Interdependence**- Team mates are made to work through a hypothetical situation to succeed and/or survive as a group. The simulation they participate in is a means of binding them to each other. (Some examples: Nuclear Attack Survival-survival activity; Restaurant team-simulation).

(ix) **Environmental Interdependence**- The physical environment facilitates the group members being bound together. (For example, mountain climbers are environmentally interdependent in that all team members are physically connected via their groups; each group has a special meeting area; requiring all group members to be within an area marked out by tapes.). The teacher has to find and create an environment that unifies students.

9. STRUCTURING INDIVIDUAL ACCOUNTABILITY

Individual accountability is the measurement of whether or not each group member has achieved the group's goal. Assessing the quality and quantity of each member's contributions and giving the results to all group members is the basic function of structuring individual accountability. It is important that the group should know that who needs more assistance, support and encouragement in completing the assignment. It is also important that group members know that they cannot "hitch hike" on the work of others.

Individual accountability is the factor that shows that students are learning better cooperatively. "The purpose of cooperative groups is to make each member a stronger individually in his or her own right". After participating in a cooperative lesson, group members should be better able to accomplish the same kind of tasks themselves. They learn to do something together so that they can do it easily when they are alone.

Lev Vygotsky (1986) also favoured this view when he said, "What children can do together today, they can do alone tomorrow". (p. 188)

To ensure that each student is individually accountable to do his or her fair share of the group's work, one needs to assess how much effort each member is contributing to the group's work, provide feedback to groups and individual students, help groups avoid redundant efforts by members, and ensure that every member is responsible for the final outcome. Common ways in which individual accountability can be structured include:

(a) Keeping the size of the group small. The smaller the size of the group, the greater the individual accountability may be.

(b) Giving an individual test to each student.

(c) Randomly examining students orally by calling on one student to present his or her group's work (in the presence of the group) or to the entire class.

(d) Observing each group and recording the frequency with which each member-contributes to the group's work.

(e) Assigning one student in each group the role of checker. The checker asks other group members to explain the reasoning and rationale underlying group answers.

(f) Having students teach what they learned to someone else. When all students do this, it is called simultaneous explaining.

There is a pattern to classroom learning. First, students learn knowledge, skills, strategies, or procedures in a cooperative group. Second, students apply the knowledge or perform the skill, strategy, or procedure alone to demonstrate their personal mastery of the material. Students learn it together and then perform it alone.

10. Structuring Intergroup Cooperation and Promotive Interaction

Positive interdependence results in promotive interaction. Promotive interaction may be defined as individuals encouraging and facilitating each other's efforts to achieve, complete tasks, and produce in order to reach the group's goals. Although positive interdependence in and of itself may have some effect on outcomes, it is the face-to-face promotive interaction among individuals fostered by the positive inter-relationships, and psychological adjustment and social competence. Promotive interaction in individuals can be enhanced by motivating them to-

(a) Provide each other with efficient and effective help and assistance,

(b) Exchange needed resources, such as information and materials, and process information more efficiently and effectively,

(c) Provide each other with feedback in order to improve their subsequent performance,

(d) Challenge each other's conclusions and reasoning in order to promote higher quality decision making and greater insight into the problems being considered,

(e) Advocate the exertion of effort to achieve mutual goals,

(f) Influence each other's efforts to achieve the group's goals,

(g) Act in trusting and trustworthy ways,

(h) Be motivated to strive for mutual benefit, and

(i) Maintain a moderate level of arousal characterized by low anxiety and stress.

11. Specifying Desired Behaviours (Interpersonal and Small Group Skills)

Another essential element of cooperative learning is the appropriate use of inter personal and small-group skills. Numerous interpersonal and small group skills affect the success of cooperative efforts. In order to coordinate efforts to achieve mutual goals, students must-

(a) Get to know and trust each other,

(b) Communicate accurately and unambiguously,

(c) Accept and support each other, and

(d) Resolve conflict constructively

Placing socially unskilled students in a group and telling them to cooperate does not guarantee that they have the ability to do so effectively. We are not born instinctively knowing how to interact effectively with others. Interpersonal and small-group skills do not magically appear when they are needed, Students have to be taught the social skills required for high quality collaboration and be motivated to use them if cooperative groups are to be productive. The whole field of group dynamics is based on the premise that social skills are the key to group productivity.

Skills Needed for Cooperative Learning

What cooperative skills are to be emphasized depends on what skills the students have and have not mastered. There are four levels of cooperative skills-

(i) Forming skills

(ii) Functioning skills

(iii) Formulating skills

(iv) Fermenting skills

(i) **Forming skills**- Forming skills are the skills needed to establish a cooperative learning group, help organize the group and establish minimum norms for appropriate behaviour. To accomplish this, students need to ensure that classmates move into cooperative learning groups quietly. ("Quietly move into your groups"); ensure that group members stay in the group and participate in the group's work. ("Stay with the group and do not wander around the room"); remind group members to use quiet voices. ("Use quiet voices"); and ensure that each student has a part in the group effort and assignment ("Lets help out each other").

(ii) **Functioning skills**- Functioning skills help the group manage their efforts and maintain working relationships. To accomplish this goal, students need to share ideas and opinions ("What is your view regarding....."); ask for facts and reasoning ("Tell me something about.....") that will ease their interaction and thus their understanding of each other's work; give direction to the group work to help the group move ahead ("We are supposed to....." or "Why don't we try this in the time we have left?"); encourage everyone to participate ("Deepa what is your opinion about this?"); ask for help or clarification ("I couldn't understand, can you explain again what you meant?"); accept support and acceptance, offer to explain and clarify ("Would you like me to explain this again?"); paraphrase ("So you mean to say that....."); energize the group ("Come on, let's get thing moving!"); and describe feelings ("I felt like.....").

(iii) **Formulating skills**- Formulating skills are needed to build deeper-level understanding of the material being studied, to stimulate the use of higher-quality reasoning strategies, and to maximize mastery and retention of the assigned material. For this the students need to summarize out loud from memory ("To sum up the concept....."); seek accuracy by correcting a member's summary ("I am not sure if this is correct...We should check....."); seek elaboration by relating the material learned to earlier learned material and to previous knowledge ("How does this relate to....."); help the group remember ("We should use colours for this table....."); check for understanding by demanding verbalization and asking the others to plan out loud ("How would you proceed with this material.....?").

(iv) **Fermenting skills**- Fermenting skills are needed for becoming involved in academic controversies, to stimulate re-conceptualization of the material being studied, cognitive conflict, the search for more information and the communication of the rationale behind one's conclusions. For this the students need to criticize ideas without criticizing people ("I respect you, but in this case

I do not agree with your approach"); differentiate between ideas and reasoning of group members ("How we differ in regard to our information and conclusions?"); integrate ideas into single positions ("Would this conclusion summarize everyone's ideas?"); ask for justifications ("Can you explain your answer?"); extend answers ("I have a little extra information about this and I want to share it with you....."); probe by asking in-depth questions ("Would it work in a different situation?"); generate further answers ("Can we consider another possibility?"); and test reality by checking the group's work.

The above mentioned skills and many more of their category, enhance communication, trust, leadership, decision-making and conflict management of the individuals.

12. TEACHING COOPERATIVE SKILLS

Engaging in an interpersonal action requires the contact opportunity with other people for the act to occur, a reason sufficient to motivate the act, and access to a method or procedure whereby the act can occur. For students to work as a team, they should be provided-

(a) An opportunity to work together cooperatively (where teamwork skills can be manifested),

(b) A motivation to engage in the teamwork skills (a reason to believe that such actions will be beneficial to them), and

(c) Some proficiency in using teamwork skills.

After providing students with the opportunity to learn in cooperative groups, one must provide students with the motive and means for doing so.

Johnson, Johnson and *Holubec* (1998) have described four steps which can be used for teaching the different social skills to the students. They are-

Step 1. Ensure that students understand the need for the teamwork skill. To establish the need for the teamwork skill, one can-

- Ask students to develop a list of social skills needed to improve group work. From the skills they list, emphasize one or two.

- Present a case to students so they can see it is better to know the skill than not to know it. Compliment the students who use the skills in the classroom.

- Illustrate the need for the skill through a role play that provides a counter-example in which the skill is obviously missing in the group.

Step 2. Ensure the students understand what the cooperative learning skill is, how, and when to use the skill. To accomplish this one can do the following-

- Define the skill in terms of verbal and non-verbal behaviors and explain thoroughly what students have to do. This can be done with a "T- chart". After listing the skill (e.g. checking for understanding) the class is asked: "What would this skill look like?" (non-verbal behaviors) and "What does this skill sound like?" (verbal behaviour).

- Demonstrate and model the skill in front of the students and explain it step by step so students have a concrete idea of what the skill entails in terms of verbal and non-verbal behaviour.

- Have the students practice the skill twice in their groups before the lesson starts.

"T-chart" that can be used to teach the social skill of 'Checking for Understanding' in the cooperative classroom-

CHECKING FOR UNDERSTANDING

Looks Like (Non Verbal)	*Sounds Like (Verbal)*
Eye contact	Explain that to me please
Leaning forward	Can you show me?
Interested expression	Tell us how to do it.
Open gestures and postures	How did you get to that conclusion?

Similar "T-charts" can be prepared for teaching different social skills.

Step 3. Set up practice situations and encourage skill mastery. To master a skill, students need to practice it again and again. Helping the students accomplish this task, one can-

- Assign a social skill either as a specific role for certain students or as a general responsibility for all members of the group. Introduce the skills gradually, for example one new skill every week and repeat the previously introduced skill at the same time until mastery occurs.
- Observe each group and record who uses the skill, how frequently and how effectively. One can begin with a very simple observation form that measures only two or three skills.
- Cue the use of skills periodically during a lesson by having a student demonstrate the skill in front of the others.
- Intervene in the cooperative groups to explain the skills and show how to use them.
- Coach the students on how to improve the use of the skill.

Step 4. Ensure effective communication in the learning process. For this provide each student with-

- Feedback on his or her use of the skill and

- Reflection on how to engage in the skill more effectively next time.

On the basis of the feedback received and their own assessment of their skill used, the students reflect on how to use the skill more effectively in the future.

Step 5. Ensure that students practice the skill until the skill seems a natural action. Students are required to pass the four stages of skill development-

- Awkward (the beginning stage, when there is awkwardness in engaging in the skill)

- Phony (when students use the skill but feel inauthentic)

- Mechanical

- Integrated (when the skill occurs naturally).

Because the students are simultaneously engaged in task work and team work, they should learn both. When specifying the expected behaviors, one should be specific in defining each social skill, start small by emphasizing no more than one or two behaviours at a time and emphasize practicing of the skills until they become automatic.

13. MONITORING STUDENTS BEHAVIOUR

To monitor means to check continuously. It is important to observe/monitor the interaction among group members to assess student's academic progress and appropriate use of interpersonal and small group skills and to see what problem are being faced by the students to complete the assignment and in working cooperatively. Observation is the main monitoring tool which can be used to assess learning and instruction. Observation is recording and describing behaviour as it occurs in classroom. Its purpose is to provide objective data about the quality of student's performance and the quality of the processes and methods students use in completing tasks. A variety of observation instruments and procedures can be used for these purposes. A formal observation sheet can be used to record the frequency of appropriate behaviour shown by the students. The more concrete the data, the more useful it is for us. While recording data on the formal observation sheet, too many different behaviors should not be taken at a time, instead initially only one or two behaviors should be observed like when observing social skills, skills like- contributing ideas, asking questions, active listening, expressing support and acceptance, encouraging group members to participate, summarizing, checking for understanding, sharing materials, expressing warmth and liking towards group and group members, giving direction to group's work, etc. may be observed. Besides observing social skills, academic learning and performance, cognitive reasoning, attitudes and work methods can also be observed. For observing students formal observation forms which are used to record the frequency of behaviour; observation checklists which are used to determine the quality of behaviour; and informal observation which is a teacher's impressions of what is happening in the classroom can be used within the classroom. While monitoring, one can collect notes on specific student behaviors so that the frequency data can be extended. All the data collected can be shared with students and perhaps with parents in conferences and meetings to analyze their progress.

14. PROVIDING TASK ASSISTANCE

While monitoring the students as they work, one may clarify instructions, review important procedures and strategies for completing the assignment answer the questions and teach task skills as and when necessary. While discussing the concepts and information to be learned language and terms relevant to the learning should be used. Instead of saying, "Yes, that is right", something more specific to the task can be said like, "Yes, that is one way to find out the answer to the problem". The use of the more specific statements reinforces the desired learning and promotes positive transfer by helping the students associate a term with their learning.

15. INTERVENING TO TEACH INTERPERSONAL SKILLS

While monitoring the learning groups, one may find students who do not have the necessary cooperative skills and groups in which problems in cooperation arise. In such cases, one may intervene to suggest more effective procedures for working together and more effective behaviors for students to engage in. When it is obvious that group members lack certain social skills necessary to cooperate with each other, one should intervene in order to help the members learn those skills. At times, one may become a consultant to a group in order to help it function more effectively. We often find that cooperative groups often work their way through their own problems (task and maintenance) and acquire not only a solution but also a method of solving similar problems in the future. Choosing when to intervene and when not to is part of the art of teaching and hence, one should judiciously use it. Intervening should leave a cooperative learning group with new skills that will be useful in the future. One should also praise and reinforce particularly the effective and skillful behaviors.

16. PROVIDING CLOSURE THROUGH SUMMARIZATION

At the end of the cooperative learning assignment, students should be able to summarize what they have learned and to understand where they would use it in future. Providing closure to the assignment, one should summarize the major points in the lesson, ask students to recall ideas or give examples and answer any final questions students have.

17. GROUP PROCESSING

An essential component of cooperative learning is group processing. Effective group work is influenced by whether or not groups periodically reflect on how well they are functioning and plan how to improve their work processes. Group processing exists when members reflect on members' interaction to clarify and improve efforts to achieve the group's goals and maintain effective working relationships by-

(a) Describing what member actions were helpful and unhelpful and

(b) Making decisions about what actions to continue or change.

Groups need specific time to describe what member actions were helpful and unhelpful and make decisions about what behaviors to continue or change. The purpose of group processing is to:

(a) Improve continuously the quality of the group's task work and teamwork.

(b) Increase individual accountability by focusing attention on each member's responsible and skillful actions to learn and to help group mates learn.

(c) Streamline the learning process to make it simpler (reducing complexity).

(d) Eliminate unskilled and inappropriate actions (error-proofing the process).

Group processing occurs at the small-group and whole-class levels. Each level comprises of four levels of processing-

(i) Feedback

(ii) Reflection

(iii) Setting Improvement Goals

(iv) Celebration

(i) **Feedback-** To begin group processing, one should ensure that learning groups and individual students receive feedback. Feedback is information on actual performance that individuals compare with criteria for ideal performance. Feedback is based on the information the teacher and students collect while monitoring the learning groups. When feedback is given skillfully, it generates energy, directs the energy towards constructive action, and transforms the energy into action towards improving the performance of the teamwork skills. When this occurs student performance is enhanced, self-efficacy increases, and students feel compelled to be more effective in the next group effort.

(ii) **Reflection-** The second step in structuring group processing is when students reflect on and analyze the group session they have just completed to discover what helped and what hindered the quality of learning and whether specific behaviors had a positive or negative effect. Varying the procedures for analyzing and reflecting on the data collected about members' interactions keeps group processing vital and interesting. It is very important for each group member to receive positive feedback for reflection. This can be done by- having each group focus on one member at a time, having members write a positive comment about each team mate on a card and having students comment on the proper use of social skills.

(iii) **Setting Improvement Goals-** The third step in structuring group processing is to encourage students to set improvement goals. After analyzing the observational and self-assessment data, reflecting on its meaning, and giving each other feedback, group members are made to set improvement goals specifying how they will act more skillfully in the next group session. Students should be made to publicly announce the behavior they plan to increase. They should write the goal down and review it at the beginning of the next group session. Goal setting is the link between how students did today and how well they will do tomorrow. Goal setting can have a powerful impact on students' behavior as there is a sense of ownership of and commitment to actions that a student has decided to engage in (as opposed to assigned behaviors).

(iv) **Celebrating-** The fourth step in structuring group processing is when group members celebrate their success and members' efforts to learn. Group processing ends with students celebrating their hard work and the success of their cooperative learning group. Celebrations are key to encouraging students to persist in their efforts to learn. Long-term, hard, persistent efforts to learn come more from the heart than from the head. Being recognized for efforts to learn and to contribute to group mates' learning reaches the heart more effectively than do grades or tangible rewards. Both small-group and whole-class celebrations should take place. Small group processing provides the means to celebrate the success of the group and reinforce the positive behaviors of group members. Individual efforts that contribute to the group's success should be recognized and encouraged. Members' actions aimed at helping group mates learn should be perceived, respected, and recognized. It is feeling successful, appreciated, and respected that builds commitment to learning, enthusiasm about working in cooperative groups, and a sense of self-efficacy about subject-matter mastery and working cooperatively with classmates.

18. Assessing, Evaluating And Reporting Student Learning

Assessment is the collection of data to make a judgment. **Evaluation** is the rendering of a judgment based on merit.

Reporting is the communication of the results of assessment and evaluation to interested audiences. Cooperative learning groups can enhance and at times are required for assessment, evaluation, and reporting—particularly when performance, authentic or total quality assessment is employed.

There are two levels of assessment and evaluation when cooperative learning is used in instruction. These levels are- the individual and the group. Individual assessment is more frequent than group assessment but both are important. Since the purpose of cooperative learning groups is to make each member a stronger individual in his or her own right, a pattern to classroom learning is created where students learn in a cooperative group, individually demonstrate their learning, and then debrief the learning in their cooperative group.

In planning assessment in a cooperative classroom, one has to check the targets to assess, check the procedures to use, and match the targets with the procedures. Three types of assessment can be used-

(a) Diagnostic assessment- that refers to students actual level of knowledge and skills,

What Is To Be Assessed	*Assessment Procedures*
Academic learning	Goal setting conferences
Reasoning process/strategies	Standardized tests
Skills and competencies	Teacher-made tests
Attitudes	Written compositions
Work habits	Oral presentations
	Projects
	Portfolios
	Observations
	Questionnaires
	Interviews
	Learning logs and journals
	Student management teams

(b) Formative assessment- that monitors student's progress toward learning goals and

(c) Summative assessment- that provides data to judge the final level of student's learning.

What is to be assessed and how is to be assessed can be understood by the following table-

The assessment of students learning can be described under the following two headings-

(a) Assessment Procedures and

(b) Grading Procedures

(a) **Assessment procedures**- The first step in conducting assessment is setting the learning goals. Once the learning goals are formulated and agreed upon, multiple forms of assessment may follow. These assessment procedures are – conferences, tests, compositions, presentations, projects, portfolios, observations, interviews, questionnaires, and learning logs and journals. Each student should fill out a chart that represents his/her learning goals. Student's commitment is very important for achieving the learning goal that specifies what is to be achieved in the future and what are the responsibilities for helping group mates learn.

(i) Conferences- The learning goals are created and discussed in three types of conferences- a goal-setting conference, a progress-assessment conference and a post-evaluation conference.

(ii) Tests and Examinations- Two kinds of tests can be used to assess student's learning- standardized and teacher-made. Tests and quizzes are given to assess how much each student knows and what students still need to learn.

(iii) Compositions and Presentations- The compositions and presentations are two of the most common procedures used for assessment. These procedures allow students to engage in the performance frequently, provide immediate and detailed feedback, lets students observe closely the work of others and see the strengths and drawbacks, and provide the labor needed for engaging in performances.

(iv) Individual and Group Projects- As an assessment procedure projects allow students to use multiple learning styles and strategies. Using these as an assessment procedure in cooperative learning enhances the complexity and elaboration of the projects as more students bring more ideas to the project.

(v) Portfolios- A portfolio as an assessment procedure is a collection of a student's work in an area, showing growth, self-reflection, and achievement. Portfolios can also show a cooperative group's progress.

(vi) Observation- while tests, compositions, projects and portfolios show whether or not students could reach the correct answer, they do not show the quality of the reasoning strategies the students use and the effective use of social skills in cooperative groups. Consequently, observation becomes one of the most important assessment procedures. There are three stages in observing students actions- prepare for observation by deciding who the observers are and what actions they are to observe, observe formal and/or informal, and summarize the results for students use.

(vii) Interview- When observing students at work, the teacher can interview them to find out about their reasoning process and strategies. The personal nature of the interview allows the teacher to build a positive relationship with the student.

(viii) Attitude Questionnaires- Obtaining good grades doesn't mean that the students really like the subject matter. To know this one has to rely on attitude questionnaires. These show the attitudes students have towards a subject area.

(ix) Logs and Journals- Learning logs and journals help students keep track and reflect on their learning experiences. Logs refer to short entries related to the subject matter being studied. Journals entries are more related to personal observations and feelings. The teacher can assign point values to both logs and journals entries.

For different assessment procedures, different rubrics have to be prepared such as rubric for assessing presentations, compositions, projects, attitudes, etc. Some of the rubrics are available in ready-to-use format while as per requirement rubrics can be prepared by the teachers also. The essence of effective assessment lies in implementing the rubrics effectively and reporting the data to interested audience.

(b) **Grading Procedures**- Some options which can be used for grading students in cooperative learning situations are as under-

(i) Individual score plus bonus points based on all members reaching criterion.

(ii) Individual score plus bonus points based on lowest score.

(iii) Individual score plus group average.

(iv) Individual score plus bonus based on improvement scores. Bonus points are awarded on the basis of whether team member's percentage on the current test is higher than the average percentage on all past tests.

(v) Summing up members individual scores. If group members scored 95, 80, 90, and 90 each student gets the score of 360.

(vi) Averaging the member's individual scores. If the member's scores are 90, 95, 85, and 90 then each group member would receive 90 points.

(vii) Group score on a single product. All group members receive the same score that is the grade obtained on a single group product.

Besides these, one can create his/her own system of grading students in a cooperative learning lesson as per requirement of the lesson.

8

Benefits of Cooperative Learning

The benefits of Cooperative Learning can be organized into three categories-academic, social and psychological.

8.1 ACADEMIC BENEFITS

Cooperative learning –

(A) PROMOTES HIGHER LEVEL THINKING SKILLS BY

1. Stimulating critical thinking and helping students to clarify ideas through discussion and debate

When students work in pairs or in three or four member teams, they listen and discus the question under investigation, one by one. Consequently they develop valuable problem solving skills by formulating their ideas, discussing them, receiving immediate feedback and responding to questions and comments by their partners. *Slavin* (1992) emphasized that students learn from one another because while discussing the content, cognitive conflicts arise, inadequate reasoning is exposed, disequilibrium occurs and thus, higher quality understandings emerge.

2. Enhancing skill building and practice

In a lecture based setting, we are limited to the extent to which we can convey skills and practices. But while working within a small group setting students are encouraged, helped by their peers and the instructor, and they learn from one another by watching and imitating. When students work together the learning process becomes interesting and fun despite the repetitive nature of the learning process.

3. Developing oral communication skills

When students work in pairs, one partner verbalizes his/ her answer while the other listens, asks questions or comments upon what he/she has heard. Three benefits occur due to this process. First, the students demonstrate the thinking process they are using. The dull students can derive help from this by knowing the ways of approaching a problem the more advance students use. Second, instead of an individual thinking about a problem in small increments, in isolation, a group often looks at a problem from a wide perspective and considers many more options as possible solutions than one person thinking alone. Third, by discussing various aspects of a problem solution and questioning the more advanced students, the novices in the group can participate in actually solving the problem and eventually learn how to solve problems without the help of peers.

4. Fostering metacognition in students

Metacognition involves student recognition and analysis of how they learn. Metacognition activities enable students to monitor the performance in a course and their comprehension of the content material. This includes detecting errors and learning how to make corrections while monitoring one's performance. Cooperative learning approaches create learning strategies which are independent of content and thus are transferable to different content areas.

Johnson and Johnson (1992) identified several practical reasons why cooperative learning, especially using their constructive controversy approach, enhances student metacognition. The fact that students are required to explain their strategies or teach other students changes the learning strategies they use compared to how to organize material when they are learning independently. Discussions within cooperative groups require more frequent oral summarizing, explaining and elaboration of what one knows which in turn consolidates and strengthens what is known through rehearsal process. The heterogeneity of cooperative groups encourages students to accommodate themselves to their peer's perspectives, strategies and approaches to complete assignments. This stimulates divergent and creative thinking and review of one's own thinking. Students often bring incomplete information to a task and by interacting with other students learn how to share their information and obtain insights on how other students obtain and use information, thus expanding their understanding of their own thinking processes. By sharing their work within cooperative groups, students externalize their ideas and reasoning for critical examination which in turn results in peer monitoring and regulation or members thinking and reasoning. Students give each other feedback regarding the quality and relevance of their contributions and make suggestions on how to improve their performance.

5. Improving students retention and recall of the content

When students read a text together and explain the concepts to each other and evaluate each other's explanations they engage in a high level of critical thinking. They frame the new concepts by using their own vocabulary and by basing their comments upon their previous knowledge. In the whole process the students construct a knowledge base on the top of their existing base which leads to deeper understanding and retention of the material for a long time.

(B) INVOLVES STUDENTS ACTIVELY IN THE LEARNING PROCESS BY

1. Creating an environment of active and exploratory learning

The entire focus of cooperative learning is to actively involve students in the learning process. When two or more students attempt to solve a problem or answer a question they become involved in the process of exploratory learning. They interact with each other, share ideas and information, seek additional information, make decisions about their deliberations and present their findings to the entire class. They may tutor their peers or receive tutoring. This is a level of student empowerment which is unattainable with a lecture format or even with a teacher-led whole class discussion.

2. Encouraging student responsibility for learning

Promotive interaction and individual accountability create a feeling of responsibility amongst the students for themselves and their group members. Students are made to assist each other and take different roles within their groups such as a reader, recorder, time keeper, etc. and while doing so an emphasis on student involvement is created. The empowerment of students produces an environment which fosters maturity and responsibility in students for their learning. The teacher becomes a facilitator instead of a director and the student becomes a willing participant instead of a passive follower.

3. Involving students in developing curriculum and class procedures

During the cooperative learning process students are asked to assess themselves, and their groups as well as class procedures. This student input can be used by the teacher to modify make up of groups or class assignments and alter the mix of lecture and group work accordingly.

Marzano (1992) identified four specific ways in which students become involved in developing class procedures when cooperative learning is in process. The class can identify desired features of the physical environment, such as arrangement of desks, display of classroom accessories, etc. students can suggest activities which will promote positive interactions or deal with conflicts or personality problems within each group. The class may be given responsibility for developing and implementing classroom rules and procedures. Students can help establish and implement rules for physical and psychological safety of the peers, such as a code of conduct which encourages students to respect each other, listen and respond attentively and generally care for their fellow students.

4. Providing training in effective teaching strategies to the next generation teachers

New teachers are likely to teach using the teaching style they have been exposed to during their education. The primary paradigm at universities is the lecture method combined with a competitive assessment process. If the probable teachers are given more exposure and practice using cooperative learning methods and are made to observe the significant benefits and students reactions they would be more inclined to obtain additional training and to try these techniques in their classes.

5. Helping students to wean themselves away from considering teachers the sole source of knowledge and understanding

Cooperative learning approaches learning from a student centered philosophy by encouraging students to take responsibility for their learning by involving students throughout the class and encouraging their collaboration in group effort outside the class. The teacher serves as a resource and facilitator rather than as an expert. It is not a passive role for the teacher because it requires a lot of planning and preparation on the part of the teacher. The goal is to begin to elevate students to the teacher's level and create a high expectation that they have the ability to obtain and understand knowledge themselves.

6. Promoting a learning goal rather than performance goal

Typical teaching paradigms consist of individual student efforts characterized by competitive testing to assess student competence. This approach leads to a performance goal as the desired outcome of the educational experience. With cooperative learning the primary focus is on the process of learning and how individuals function within groups and independently, but not necessarily competitively. Cooperative learning is student centered versus teacher centered leading to a stronger emphasis on the goal of learning. It encourages teachers to use alternate assessment techniques further reducing the emphasis on competitive examinations.

7. Conjugating well with the constructivist approach

Only when students formulate their own constructs and solutions are they truly thinking critically. Cooperative learning techniques create a constructivist approach when students become actively involved in defining questions in their own language and working out answers together instead of reproducing material presented by the teacher or the text book.

8. Allowing students to exercise a sense of control on task

The interactive nature of cooperative learning exercises places the students in a position of control over the process and encourages them to take full responsibility for the outcome of particular assignment. Students receive training in social skill building, conflict resolution and team management. Students are given a great deal of freedom to decide how they will function and what their group's product will be. Cooperative learning empowers students to take control over their education.

(C) IMPROVES CLASSROOM RESULTS BY

1. Promoting higher achievement and class attendance

When cooperative learning is structured within classrooms, students develop personal professional relations with teachers by getting to know them. Teachers also get to know their students and understand their problems and can find ways of dealing with those problems. Students are often inspired by the teacher who takes time to get to know them and encourage them to aspire to better performance.

According to *Felder* (1997) additional benefits occur in that student grades are improved, they show longer retention of information, transfer information better to other courses and disciplines and have better class attendance.

2. Promoting a positive attitude towards the subject matter

Cooperative learning fosters a higher level of performance by students. Their critical thinking skills increase and the retention of information and interest in the subject matter improves. When students are successful they view the subject matter with a very positive attitude because their self esteem is enhanced. This creates a positive cycle of good performance building higher self esteem which in turn leads to more interest in the subject matter and yet higher performance.

3. Enhancing self management skills

Cooperative learning inherently calls for self management by students. In order to function within their groups they need to come prepared with assignments completed and they must understand the material they are going to contribute to the group. Students are given training about their responsibilities toward the group and how to be effective group member. The promotive interactions within the group help students learn self management techniques. From a psychological view cooperative learning fosters self efficacy among students. Student self direction is generated in part by the high expectations by the teacher and the high degree of responsibility placed upon the students for their learning.

4. Motivating students to stay on task and be less disruptive

An enormous hidden benefit of cooperative learning is one most attractive to teachers: it negates many forms of student disruptive behaviour. Studies have shown that students engage in disruptive behaviour because they need peer interaction in the learning process for their own cognitive and social development. If the context is highly non interactive, students look for legitimized and non-legitimized avenues for interactions. This off-task interaction is perceived by teachers as an indication of growing discipline problems. For the students, however, it helps fulfill their need for interaction. If interaction is not channeled into legitimate processes, it emerges as social events. Small group cooperative learning structures prove to be mechanisms which provide academic student interactions within social contexts. So students remain focused on their task and chances of disruptive behaviour by students are minimized.

5. Promoting innovation in teaching and classroom techniques

Cooperative learning processes include class warm up activities, name recognition games, group building activities and group processing. Students work in pairs or larger groups depending upon the task at hand. Group work on content takes any forms such as individual questions, problem assignments, projects, study activities, group tests, etc. classes are interesting and enjoyable because of the variety of the activities available for use by the teacher. Cooperative learning effectively and actively involves students in the learning process and can be easily integrated with other teaching strategies.

(D) MODELS APPROPRIATE STUDENT PROBLEM SOLVING TECHNIQUES BY

1. Improving performance of weaker students when they are grouped with higher achieving students

One reason for the improvement may be explained by the intense one on one tutoring which is possible with cooperative learning. Another explanation offered by *Johnson and Johnson* (1990) is that weaker students are given the opportunity to model the reasoning processes of stronger students as well as preparing each other for tests, checking and correcting home work, etc. also social interaction according to Vygotsky, extends the students zone of proximal development which increases their ability to solve problems.

2. Providing stronger students with the deeper understanding that comes only from teaching material

The student who does the explaining is the student who benefits. High achievers benefit from participation in heterogeneous groups especially by giving explanations to others because the process of explaining one's reasoning creates a higher level of conceptual understanding and promotes critical thinking skills.

3. Leading to the generation of more and better questions in class

The use of group brainstorming techniques in cooperative learning classes create an environment which stimulates questioning by students during class. *Felder* (1997) suggested a procedure where teams of three are asked to take one minute to come up with three good questions about what was just discussed in class. By sharing information in class the teacher and students gain much better understanding of what they learned and what material needs to be covered in future classes.

4. Enabling students to explore alternate problem solutions in a safe environment

Many students are hesitant to speak out and offer opinions publicly in a traditional classroom setting for fear of appearing foolish. When students work in groups, solutions come from the group rather than from the individual. Students can propose ideas and theories to their peers prior to formulating a final response, and then rehearse their presentation in an informal setting. Thus, cooperative learning creates a safe, nurturing environment, where students can express themselves and explore their ideas without the fear of failure or criticism. In a lecture format an individual student responds to a question before the entire class without much time to think about his/her answer; such a situation creates a threatening environment.

5. Addressing learning style differences among students

Students working in cooperative classes utilize each of the three main learning styles: kinesthetic, auditory and visual. Each of these learning styles is addressed many times throughout a class in contrast to the lecture format which is mainly auditory and occasionally visual.

(E) PERSONALIZES LARGE LECTURE CLASSES BY

1. Breaking the lecture into more manageable and understandable segments

By having students work in pairs teachers can overcome some of the limitations created by the lecture method. Even in a large lecture students can be asked to turn to a neighbour and discuss a question posed by the teacher, write a consensus summary of the lecture or made to participate in any number of short cooperative activities. This approach personalizes the class by creating an atmosphere of interaction among students. It breaks the lecture into more manageable and understandable segments. It places some of the responsibility for the class content with the student and helps student reflect upon what they are learning and creates an opportunity for students to ask questions or clarify difficult concepts.

2. Involving students in interactive thinking activities during class

It is nearly impossible to lead a whole class discussion in large lecture classrooms, however it is possible to give students a critical thinking task by having them work with neighbour for ten minutes or so and then asking representative groups to present and justify their solutions. This technique creates an active learning environment and also gives the teacher immediate feedback on the material presented. On the other hand, in lecture method, students listen to the teacher, take notes and then leave the class to decipher what was said on their own. Cooperative structures developed by *Kagan*, are a boon to teachers who want to experiment with cooperative learning.

(F) FACILITATES TRANSFER OF LEARNING BY

1. Providing a class set-up almost similar to the real professional world

Kohn (1992) and *Caroselli* (1998) observed that working in teams in the classrooms encourages flexibility and adaptability, promotes student socialization, thus, aiding in the transition of students to professional in an increasingly diverse commercial industry.

8.2 SOCIAL BENEFITS

Cooperative Learning-

(A) DEVELOPS A SOCIAL SUPPORT SYSTEM FOR STUDENTS BY

1. Promoting student-faculty interaction and familiarity

The cooperative process enables the teacher to move around the class in order to observe students interacting. An opportunity is created whereby the teacher can talk to the students directly or in small groups. Openings like this lead to a discussion of problems by the teacher and student in a non-threatening way because of the informality of the situation.

2. Developing social interaction skills

A major component of cooperative learning elaborated by *Johnson, Johnson and Holubec* (1984) includes training students in the social skills needed to work cooperatively. Students do not come by these skills naturally. Quite the contrary, in our society and current educational framework competition is valued over cooperation. By asking group members to identify what behaviours help them work together and by asking individuals to reflect on their contribution to the group's success or failure, students are made aware of the need for healthy, positive, helping interactions when they work in groups.

3. Promoting positive societal responses to problems and fosters a supportive environment within which to manage conflict resolution

Research shows that cooperative learning reduces violence in any setting. It trains students to be peace makers. As elaborated by *Staub* (2002) the aims of peace education are to develop caring and non-aggressive individuals who relate peacefully to others in their own lives, who promote the welfare of others and who takes action to prevent violence in their society and in the world. Cooperative learning teaches all students in our schools the knowledge, procedural competencies, identity and values required to maintain peace within themselves, (intrapersonal peace) among individuals, (interpersonal peace) among groups, (inter group peace) and among countries, societies and cultures (international peace). Through cooperative learning students learn attitudes, concepts and competencies that generalize across all levels of conflict resolution from interpersonal to international and that may even relate to intrapersonal conflict, democratic and tolerant attitudes, concepts like interdependency and reciprocity and competencies for empathy, impulse control, problem solving and negotiation. In essence it attempts to develop a set of behavioural skills necessary for peaceful living and peace-building from which the whole of humanity will benefit.

4. Fostering and developing interpersonal relationships

The social nature of cooperative learning process improves interpersonal relationships among students. It encourages out of class work by the groups, bringing them together in a combined academic and social experience which continues over long periods of time.

5. Developing responsibility amongst students for each other

In a traditional competitive class students are concerned with their individual grades. In the cooperative class the opposite is true. A nurturing atmosphere is created whereby students help each other and take responsibility for their entire group's work. Group celebration of individual and group performance promotes a supportive atmosphere and highlights each student's responsibility to the entire group.

(B) BUILDS DIVERSITY UNDERSTANDING AMONG STUDENTS AND STAFF BY

1. Building more positive heterogeneous relationships

The current educational system rewards student's achievement by separating students of differing abilities rather than encouraging students to utilize their abilities to help each other. Research has shown that when students of high ability work with students of lower ability both benefit, the former by explaining and the latter by seeing a concept modeled by a peer. Both observe each other's approaches to problem solving and begin to appreciate their differences.

2. Fostering a greater ability in students to view situations from others perspective

Due to continuous interaction between students during cooperative learning a much deeper understanding of individual differences and cultural differences among students is developed. Cooperative learning helps majority and minority populations in a class learn to work with each other. Because students are actively involved in exploring issues and interacting with each other on a regular basis in a guided fashion, they are able to understand the differences and learn how to resolve social problems which may arise. Cooperative learning promotes development of empathy in students.

(C) ESTABLISHES A POSITIVE ATMOSPHERE FOR MODELING AND PRACTICING COOPERATION BY

1. Establishing an atmosphere of cooperation and helping

Most schools celebrate individual student performance through athletics, clubs or extra curricular activities even when these accomplishments are the result of team efforts. In contrast, cooperative learning focuses attention on the accomplishments of the group. Students are trained how to interact positively, resolve disputes through compromise and/or mediation and encourage the best performance of each member for the benefit of the group. Teamwork is the modus operandi and inter group cooperation is encouraged.

2. Teaching students how to criticize ideas not people

A function of cooperative learning is to help students resolve differences amicably. They need to be taught how to challenge ideas and advocate for their positions without personalizing their statements. They are also taught conflict resolution methods, which are important for real life situations as well as being useful for academic endeavors.

3. Providing for desirable social behaviours necessary for employment situations which utilize teams and groups

Students socialize with family members and friends and work in situations which require team work and group work. Training in cooperative learning followed by group activities and processes provide an environment in which student can practice building good social skills, process beneficial group behaviour and generally observe each other's actions and reactions to their behaviours.

4. Allowing students practice modeling of societal and work related roles

In cooperative classes students are assigned roles in order to build interdependence within the groups such as reader, recorder, reporter, materials handler, time keeper, etc. which are rotated among group members for each new assignment or project. Students are thus encouraged to develop and practice the skills which will be needed to function in society and the work world. These skills include leadership, information recording, and communication of results orally and in writing, challenging ideas in a constructive manner, obtaining and distributing materials and information to group members, encouraging group participation, brainstorming, meeting deadlines, etc. Students are made to realize the direct applicability of classroom small group problem solving to their own lives which motivates them and enhances their learning.

5. Fostering team building and a team approach to problem solving while maintaining individual accountability

A major function of cooperative learning is team building. This is accomplished through a variety of techniques used throughout the duration like warm up activities, getting to know class members, group building exercises, group processing, etc. which help students understand how to function in a group. Regarding individual accountability, at the end of each content section an exam or paper or other assessment technique is used to determine how well individual students have mastered the material. Group projects or group tests are given in addition. Quizzes term are also given individually to maintain a strong element of accountability by each group member. Numerous grading schemes exist which bring both elements together such as providing bonus points for group members when the group exceeds its previous group average on a test by a specified amount.

6. Creating an environment where students can practice building leadership skills

In order to help students learn how to function effectively in groups specific activities need to be employed. The assignment of different roles helps in this. The role of reader is considered to be the primary leadership role with responsibility for initially reading the material, ascertaining whether all the members understand their charge and overseeing the progress of the group, etc. the recorder has also a leadership role in insuring that the material written represents the group's thorough analysis of the problem including consensus conclusions, etc. Cooperative learning is also particularly effective at increasing leadership skills of female students and for getting male students used to turning to women for help in pressure situations.

(D) DEVELOPS LEARNING COMMUNITIES BY

1. Providing foundation within institutions and in courses

Vincent Tinto (1997) reiterated that through cooperative learning, first, students become more actively involved in classroom learning. Second, new students spend more time learning together raising their quality of learning. Third, these students form social groups outside the classrooms, bonding in ways which increase their persistence in schools and colleges. Fourth, learning communities enable students to bridge the large divide between social conduct that frequently characterize student life. They tend to learn and make close friends at the same time.

2. Promoting social and academic relationships well beyond the classroom

There is significant benefit to cooperative learning which is not apparent because it takes place outside of the classroom. When groups continue long enough during course they get to know each other and extend their activities outside class. This includes meeting off campus for meals or coffee, forming study groups, getting together at each others home in the evening and weekends to work on projects or problems they are having. Students are able to make up new friends and establish study groups easier within a cooperative learning environment.

3. Helping teachers change their roles from their being the focus of the teaching process to becoming facilitators of the learning process

Cooperative learning paradigms represent a philosophy of life as well as a learning strategy. It says that whenever people get together in groups their purposes are best served when they work together cooperatively to reach their goals versus using competition among group members to address problems. In order to bring change in current educational system, cooperative learning structures need to be introduced at the earliest starting in preschool through kindergarten and higher education. In cooperative learning the role of teacher changes from the sage on the stage and they step down from the podium and switch from lecturing to facilitating student interactions in class. For this they use different cooperative learning structures and strategies. Effective cooperative teachers continually modify their activities and adopt new structures to deal with different classroom situations and populations.

8.3 PSYCHOLOGICAL BENEFITS

Cooperative Learning-

(A) INCREASES STUDENT SELF ESTEEM BY

1. Enhancing student experience with the learning experience

By their very nature people find satisfaction with activities which value their abilities and include them in the process. When individuals are encouraged to work together towards a common goal, as a team they take up the ownership of the process and its results. This aspect is very helpful for individuals who have a history or failure.

2. Promoting a mastery attribution pattern rather than helpless attribution pattern

In a typical class students are given lectures, they complete assignments and take an exam to demonstrate their knowledge retention of the subject matter. This process is repeated over and over. There is little time for reflection and discussion of student's errors or misconceptions. On the other hand with cooperative learning, students continuously discuss debate and clarify their understanding of the concepts and materials considered in the class. They construct their own knowledge base. Assessment may vary from individual activities such as tests or oral reports to group tests or projects. The emphasis is on understanding the material as evidenced by the student's ability to explain ideas to their peers. This leads to a sense of mastery of content versus a passive acceptance of information from an outside expert who promotes a sense of helplessness and reliance upon others to attain concepts.

3. Encouraging students to seek help and accept tutoring from their peers

Students are often reluctant to seek out extra help or tutoring from their peers because help seeking is interpreted negatively as an indicator of dependency, self perceptions of low ability, embarrassment or feeling of indebt ness. *Hertz-Lazarowitz* (1992) pointed out that a person who received help when working as a member of a cooperative group expressed more liking for a teammate who provided help. This effect occurs because group setting create norms of responsibility toward teammates which minimizes the negative effects that ordinarily occur when one is unable to reciprocate help that is received. In addition group members often have opportunities to help each other thus reducing the perception of one way help.

4. Creating a more positive attitude towards teachers, principals and other personnel by students and creates a more positive attitude by teachers towards their students

The level of involvement of all the participants in cooperative system is very intense and personal. Students get to know teachers personally. Teachers learn about student behaviours because students have many opportunities to explain themselves to the teacher. Line of communication are opened and actively encouraged. Teachers have more opportunities to explain why policies are established and the system allows students to have more input into establishing policies and class procedures. The empowerment created by the many interpersonal interactions leads to a very positive attitude by all parties involved.

(B) REDUCES ANXIETY BY

1. Significantly reducing classroom anxiety

In a traditional classroom when a teacher calls upon a student, he/she becomes the focus of attention of the entire class. Any mistakes or incorrect answers become subject to scrutiny by the whole class. Such experiences produce embarrassment and anxiety in many students. In contrast, in a cooperative learning situation, when students work in a group, the focus of attention is diffused among the group. When the answer is presented to the class it represents the work of the entire group; therefore no single individual can be held up to criticism. In addition, the members can review the answer prior to presenting it to the whole class, thus, diminishing the prospects of any mistakes. Even then if a mistake is made, it becomes a teaching tool instead of a public criticism of an individual student. So, classroom anxiety is reduced as the general class attitude is one of cooperation and nurturing, not criticism.

2. Significantly reducing test anxiety

Competition increases anxiety as students are under pressure to perform. Cooperative learning creates the opposite response from students. It provides many opportunities for alternate forms of student assessment which leads to a reduction in test anxiety because the students see that the teacher is able to evaluate how they think as well as what they know. Students are not locked in a testing format which requires memorization and reproduction of basic skills. This type of atmosphere is completely lacking in a lecture class.

(C) ENHANCES OVERALL PSYCHOLOGICAL HEALTH BY

1. Developing, maintaining and appropriately modifying interdependent relationships with others to succeed in achieving goals

Johnson and Johnson (1989) indicated that cooperative attitudes are highly correlated with a wide variety of indices of psychological health such as emotional maturity, well adjusted social relations, strong personal identity, ability to cope with adversity, social competencies and basic trust and optimism about people. Cooperative experiences promote higher self esteem than do competitive (effect size=0.58) or individualistic (effect size=0.44) experiences as given by *Johnson and Johnson* (1989).

There may be no other instructional strategy that simultaneously achieves such diverse outcomes and moreover a meta analysis of all studies (Johnson and Johnson, 1989) found that the average person cooperating performed at about two-third a standard deviation above the average person learning within a competitive (effect size=0.67) or individualistic situation (effect size=0.64).

9

Teacher's Role and Concerns in Cooperative Learning

Teacher's major role in cooperative learning is that of a very good planner and facilitator. Perfect planning is required at the pre implementation phase, implementation phase and post implementation phase. The teacher needs to specify objectives, both academic and social skills. Group size is another decision the teacher has to make keeping the time limit, student's experience in working in groups, student's age, and the availability of the appropriate materials available into consideration. The teacher can assign students to groups using a random or stratified random procedure to make groups heterogeneous. When assigning group roles, the teacher needs to be sure each group includes students that possess four types of skills: forming skills, functioning skills, formulating skills and fermenting skills. The room arrangement is very important for lesson development. Teachers can use different strategies to define the workspace boundaries in a classroom. For instance a teacher could define boundaries by-using labels and signs that designate areas, using colours to attract visual attention and define group and individual spaces, taping lines on the floor to define the different work areas, moving furniture, etc. the teacher also decides how materials need to be arranged and distributed among group members to maximize their participation and achievement. The teacher creates material interdependence, information interdependence and interdependence from outside enemies by structuring materials into an inter group competition and having groups compete to see who has learned the most.

After planning the lesson by making pre instructional decisions, the teacher shapes the cooperative structure by explaining the academic task, specifying the criteria for success, explaining positive interdependence, structuring individual accountability, structuring inter group cooperation, and specifying expected behaviours. The teacher needs to tell the class what to do to complete the assignment and how to do it and what will the students get as reward for their work. First, the teacher structures positive goal interdependence and then supplements it with other types of positive interdependence such as-reward, role, resource or identity to create peer encouragement and support for learning. The teacher then needs to structure individual accountability by using different ways such as keeping group size small, giving an individual test to each student, giving random individual oral examinations, observing and recording the frequency with which each student contributes to the group's work, etc. Class goals as well as group goals and individual goals are also to be established by the teacher. In cooperative learning the teacher has to specify desired behaviours such as small group and interpersonal skills. Because students are simultaneously engaged in task work and teamwork, they must learn both. The teacher has to be specific by defining each social skill, not more than one or two at a time and emphasize over learning by having the students practice the skills until they become automatic. While conducting a lesson, the teacher monitors each learning group, intervenes when needed to improve task work and teamwork, and bring closure to the lesson.

After the implementation phase, assessing and evaluating the quantity and quality of student's learning is another very important task of the teacher. Regarding group processing, the teacher makes sure that all students receive feedback on their work, analyze the data on group functioning, set an improvement goal, and participate in a team celebration.

To keep track of what is going on, the teacher needs to fill out a cooperative learning progress report which helps the teacher make decisions regarding instruction when using cooperative learning elements. It can also serve as an evaluation tool.

While implementing any instructional strategy the major concerns of many teachers are classroom management, classroom control and classroom discipline. Within most traditional classrooms there are students who are resistant to teacher influence, unmotivated to learn what is being taught, non responsive to the usual rewards teacher have to offer and inappropriately aggressive, hostile, obstructive, irritating and disobedient. Controlling and disciplining these students is a major concern for most teachers. Yet the results of research on cooperation show a way to minimize such problems.

The inappropriate, non responsive and obstructive behaviour by students is reduced and controlled by the appropriate use of cooperation. In a cooperative situation students work together to achieve mutual goals and, therefore, are susceptible to influence from each other. This mutual influence results in more peer encouragement for achievement and a climate more oriented toward academic involvement. Instead of approval and support for learning coming from the teacher, it comes from peers. Instead of a student demonstrating independence from adults by disobeying the teacher, a student demonstrates concern for the peers by helping the group achieve. A student who doesn't care what grade the teacher assigns for his/her work cares a great deal about how his/her peers view the quality of his/her effort. Hostility towards authority is not expressed when working cooperatively with one's peers. Thus, a teacher can identify unmotivated, non responsive, obstructive students and place them rightly in cooperative relationships in which there is positive per influence.

Most traditional classrooms have students who are isolated because of their shyness, depression, or negative self-attitudes or because for one reason or another students have taken a dislike to them. Teachers are often concerned as to how to help such students, how to integrate them more fully into classroom life. Again the element of judicious heterogeneous grouping comes to the rescue of the teacher. The shy students can be placed in the groups comprising of supportive, talkative, extrovert students, free of any prejudices. The structuring of positive interdependence especially resource and role interdependence should be done skillfully by the teacher so that there is maximum, compulsory interaction among students. It reduces isolation of all. Cooperative interaction results in positive interpersonal relationships characterized by mutual liking, positive attitudes toward each other, mutual concern, friendliness, and attentiveness. When the isolated student contributes to group efforts and realizes that his resources are being utilized by the group, the mere feeling of it promotes his/her positive self-attitude and success experience. Even when students dislike each other intensely, view each other in negative ways, or want to avoid contact with each other, cooperation in achieving several mutually desired goals defined by the teacher produces mutual liking and appreciation. Thus, a teacher can reduce isolation by encouraging cooperation and interaction among students.

Another major problem for teachers is the mediating role they are required to play in conflicts among students. There are two basic principles to remember in dealing with student-student conflicts. First, the overuse and inappropriate use of competition produces conflicts among students and second, cooperative experiences reduce conflict among students. The teachers who have students who are regularly in conflict with each other can place the students in the same group and have them cooperate on a series of projects and thus avoid inappropriate conflict. The teacher can also provide a special conflict resolution area within the class where the students can meet personally, interact with each other, put their hearts out, come to an agreement, have a fair deal or resolve conflict through compromise. The teacher or any other peer can act as a facilitator in the process. Sometimes when students who are unaccustomed to cooperative work are made to work together various types of conflicts can break out. Power struggles over who is to dominate the group, division between male and female members, and other types of conflicts can occur. When intra group conflicts occur the teacher can review the positive interdependence, individual accountability and remind students of the critical elements to refocus and cooperate more effectively. The teacher can also increase processing. Having one member observe the group work and then having the group discuss the results often generates the problem solving necessary to resolve the conflict.

Spencer Kagan during his work on cooperative learning has spent a good time to design methods which ensure that no downsides occur while working with cooperative learning. The largest chapter of his basic book on cooperative learning is on social skills. It deals with issues like what to do with difficult clients, the student who refuses to work with others, the rejected student, the hostile student, the shy student, and so on. The reason he cites for devoting so much attention to the social skills is that students today are not socialized like those of the prior generations. Many do not come to school with basic politeness, caring about the needs and feelings of others, or the ability to control impulses. So, when students are placed in groups, there is potential for all sorts of social interaction problems. Cooperative learning does not create the lack of social skills, it unmasks it.

Spencer Kagan has given six keys to successful cooperative learning:

1. How to form teams (Teams)

2. How to create the will among students to work together (Will)

3. How to manage the cooperative classroom (Manage)

4. How to foster social skills (Social Skills)

5. How to make sure there is Positive Interdependence, Individual Accountability, Equal Participation, and Simultaneous Interaction (PIES), and

6. How to structure the social interaction within groups to maximize different types of positive outcomes (Structures).

As *Spencer Kagan* puts it, "Teams Will Manage Social Skills and PIES through Structures." A teacher needs all six keys to avoid the pitfalls which can occur during cooperative learning. Implementing cooperative learning depends on adopting an attitude of experimentation, the fine-tuning of cooperative learning procedures to integrate them into the teacher's style and situation, and overcoming roadblocks to implementation. Without experimentation, fine-tuning, and overcoming roadblocks, no new teaching practice can be implemented.

10

Need of Cooperative Learning in Present Times

Without the cooperation of its members society cannot survive, and the society of man has survived because the cooperativeness of its members made survival possible.....It was not an advantageous individual here and there who did so, but the group. In human societies the individuals who are most likely to survive are those who are best enabled to do so by their group.

(*Ashley Montagu*, 1965)

Cooperation is as basic to humans as the air we breathe. The ability of all students to work cooperatively with others is the keystone to building and maintaining stable marriages, families, careers, friendships and communities. It does no good to train an engineer, secretary, accountant, mechanic or teacher if the person does not have the cooperative skills needed to apply the knowledge and technical skills such as reading, speaking, listening, writing, computing and problem solving in cooperative relationships on the job, in the family and community and with friends.

It is no longer effective for teachers to use a single-strategy, purely teacher-dominated instructional method. Using a traditional "teacher -telling," "student-listening" approach helps in mass production of stereotyped learners who are theoretically sound but practically, lagging way behind their counterparts taught using different strategies which actively involve students. In every classroom, no matter what the subject area or age of the students, teachers should structure lessons so that students:

- Work cooperatively in small groups, ensuring that all members master the assigned material.
- Engage in a win-lose struggle to see who is best.
- Work independently on their own learning goals at their own pace and in their own space to achieve a preset criterion of excellence.

The way in which teachers' structure interdependence among students learning goals determines how students interact with each other- which, in turn, largely determine the cognitive and affective outcomes of instruction. An essential instructional skill that all teachers need is knowing how and when to structure students learning goals cooperatively, competitively and individualistically. Each goal structure has its place. In an ideal classroom all three goal structures would be appropriately used. All students would learn how to work cooperatively with others, compete for fun and enjoyment and work on their own. Students would work on instructional tasks within the goal structure that is most productive for the type of task and instructional objectives. It is the teacher who decides which goal structure to implement within each instructional activity. No aspect of teaching is more important than the appropriate use of goal structures.

Each teacher needs to answer the following three questions:

- Do we need to educate students to be winners? Is this a dog-eat-dog competitive world in which only the fittest survive and therefore students need to be tough competitors?

- Do we need to educate students to be rugged individualists? Does everyone need to be able to survive on his own, to live without bending to the roar of the crowd? OR

- Do we need to educate students to work with others under the discipline imposed by a common task and purpose? Is striving towards common goals the most important and pervasive activity of educated persons? Is it true that civilization exists only while humans strive to achieve common goals?

Teachers have to choose a goal structure for each lesson they teach. The three goal structures are not in competition with each other. Each goal structure has its place. In an ideal classroom all three are used. This does not mean, however, that they will all be used equally. The basic foundation of instruction, the underlying context on which all instruction rests, is cooperation. Unless used within a context of cooperation, competitive and individualistic instructions lose much of their effectiveness.

But the words cooperative and collaborative, meaning working together for a common cause, are alien to our country where the education system is based upon the concepts of rugged individualism and competition. Images of classroom filled with wooden desks, which are perfectly aligned in permanent rows, reflect this culture. In our country, of the three interaction patterns (Individualistic, Competitive and Cooperative), competitive is presently the most dominant. Research indicates that a vast majority of students view education as a competitive enterprise where one tries to do better than other students.

Cooperation among students who celebrate each other's success, encourage each other to do homework and learn to work together regardless of ethnic backgrounds or whether they are male or female, bright or struggling, disabled or not is still rare. Our education system is still based on the old paradigm of teaching and learning where knowledge is transferred from teacher to passive students, a competitive organizational structure is maintained and where education is imparted within a context of impersonal relationships among students and between teachers and students. Teacher-student and student-materials interaction, however, are not the only forms of interaction within instructional situations. The interaction that influences student's performance in instructional situations the most is student-student interaction. From the very beginning we sow the seeds of competition and individualism and then when the seeds begin to bloom we want fruits of cooperation. This is the major ambiguity in our educational system. We have to reap what we sow! The social structure within the educational institutions is out of synchrony with the social skill needs of our society and our lives. Alternatively, the situation should be reverse. Cooperation should be the forest cover and competitive and individualistic learning be the individual trees.

AT PRIMARY EDUCATION LEVEL

When a child first comes to a structured educational setting, teacher's goal is to-

- Help the child move from being aware only of himself or herself to becoming aware of other children.

- Make the child learn to share, take turns and showing caring behavior for others.

- Promote positive feelings toward school, teachers and peers.

Contrary to this, common practice in schools today has teachers striving to separate students from one another and have them work on their own. Teacher's continually use phrases like-

"Don't look at each other's papers!"

"I want to see what you can do, not your neighbor!"

"Work on your own!"

"If you talk to your friend in the class again, I'll make you write 100 times- I will not talk in the class again!"

Only competitive and individualistic learning patterns are promoted within the classrooms where as cooperative learning is totally overlooked.

"TWO HEADS LEARN BETTER THAN ONE"

According to *Glaser,* children's motivation to work in primary school level is dependent on the extent to which their basic psychological needs are met.

So, teachers should adopt such practices which promote cooperation, to bring about the desired outcomes because cooperation can provide opportunities for sharing ideas, learning how others think and react to problems and practicing oral language skills.

Research suggests that when teachers at the primary level use cooperative interaction/ learning in classroom-

- Students achieve more than in competitive or individualistic interaction.
- Students feel less anxious and more willing to take on tasks.

- Students feel more motivated to make the effort needed to maximize learning.
- Students are more positive about school, subject areas, and teachers.
- Students are more positive about each other regardless of differences in ability, ethnic background, handicapped or not.
- Students develop oral communication skills
- Students attendance is increased
- Performance of weaker students is increased when they are grouped with more able ones.
- Students satisfaction with the learning experience is enhanced.
- Students psychological health is improved.

Success in learning depends not just on cognitive factors, such as the way that information is presented, but also on the environment in which instruction takes place and students' own perception of the educational context they find themselves in. Therefore, affective factors, such as anxiety, motivation and attitudes, demand attention in any approach to pedagogy.

So early childhood educators should employ cooperative learning strategies in their instruction because cooperative learning experiences increase the probability of children's success throughout their school years.

AT SECONDARY EDUCATION LEVEL

As we know, *Bloom* identified three domains of educational activities- cognitive, affective and psychomotor. Cognitive is for mental skills, affective is for growth in feelings or emotional areas (attitude), while psychomotor is for manual or physical skills. This taxonomy of learning behaviours can be thought of as "the goals of the training process." That is after the training session, the learner should have acquired these skills. But in present competitive / individualistic educational system, the emphasis is only on the cognitive domain whereas the affective domain lies neglected and no efficient methods are utilized to develop these skills. In such a situation, the aim of "all round development" of student's personality is not fulfilled. Such a system has its dangers- dangers which are not theoretical but exhibited in practice. It equips students to secure specialized ability in algebra, biology, physics, and chemistry but not with kind of intelligence which directs ability to useful ends. Books and lectures maybe useful for teaching knowledge, comprehension and application but they are insufficient in developing critical thinking, reasoning and problem solving. These behaviours require interaction with others as well as oneself to unleash the motivation required for thinking and performing in complex ways.

Considering the present scenario, where educators are faced with a number of issues that concern ensuring that schools and educational institutions are "world class", it has now become a necessity that we adopt Cooperative Learning.

Additionally, discussion of brain based learning and teaching and multiple intelligence recommends moving away from the basic pattern of individualistic/competitive types of instruction to instructional practices that are more interactive and cooperative. The multiple intelligences are familiar concepts to secondary school teachers and many University professors especially those in teacher education. The majority of educators have also heard of *Daniel Coleman* and the concept termed 'Emotional Intelligence'. *Coleman's* (1995) research supports the claim that Emotional Intelligence, even more than Intelligence Quotient, is the most reliable predictor of success in education and in life. Ordinarily, teachers do not place priority on developing their student's emotional intelligence or social skills. They expect their students to already possess these qualities. Too often, students are not taught these skills in their families due to radical change in the relative potency of the family for the socialization of prosocial values. At the same time, the educational institutions include remarkably fewer opportunities for prosocial socialization of the students. In typical classrooms, students sit quietly and listen to the teachers; hence, little prosocial socialization occurs. Furthermore, overlooking and neglecting all these aspects, students are expected to expand their emotional intelligence and improve their social skills as they progress, but with no special training in these areas. Our society's culture and reward systems have been oriented toward competitive and individualistic work rather than cooperative work. Students not only at secondary level but in all grade levels including college, frequently have difficulty in communicating, taking turns, exchanging ideas, sharing, making requests, discussing ideas, and treating each other with respect. Until students are taught these social skills, any other efforts are destined to fail. Youngsters who lack social and emotional competence frequently experience behaviour problems and failure in academic pursuits. The lack of self-restraint and compassion for others causes them to withdraw from social interactions or turn to violent acts. Helping students develop socially and emotionally is equally important if not more important as helping them to progress academically.

Cooperative Learning has all the essential ingredients that can bring about a qualitative change in education because it is based on new paradigm of teaching which considers that knowledge is constructed, discovered, transformed and extended by students,. Education is a personal transaction among students and between teachers and students as they work together and that teacher efforts are aimed at developing student's competencies and talents. It assumes teaching to be a complex application of theory and research. Hence, it equally takes into account the cognitive as well as affective domains of learning. It lays emphasis on the mastery of knowledge, comprehension, application, analysis, synthesis and evaluation of materials under cognitive domain as well as takes into account all the five major categories of affective domain which includes the manner in which we deal with things emotionally, such as feelings, values, appreciation, enthusiasm, motivation and attitudes. When Cooperative Learning is used as a method of curriculum transaction, students exhibit following behaviours under the different categories of affective domain.

They become active participants, exhibit awareness, willingness to hear and respond, question new ideals, concepts, models, etc. in order to fully understand them, demonstrate belief in the democratic process, become sensitive towards individual and cultural differences (value diversity), show the ability to solve problems, recognize the need for balance between freedom and responsible behaviour, accept responsibility for one's behaviour, accept professional ethical standards, create a life plan in harmony with abilities, interests, and beliefs, prioritize time effectively to meet the needs of the organization, family, and self, exhibit adjustment at personal, social, emotional level, show self-reliance when working independently and cooperate in group activities (display teamwork) using an objective approach in problem solving.

All these overt behaviour bring about a change in learner which is qualitative in nature. These changes are observable and can be assessed. Developing these skills in learners is difficult following the old paradigm of teaching.

AT HIGHER EDUCATION LEVEL

If we take a glimpse of our colleges and Universities we see that as the day breaks Campus starts becoming a hub of activities.... Students are seen moving from one lecture room to another.... With their lecture notebooks firmly and safely lodged in their bags as their prized possession. As the time of their class approaches... and as soon as the professor is seen approaching, they grab their seats in the lecture hall prepared with their arms and ammunition- the 'mighty pen' to jot down the notes delivered through an information packed lecture. When the lecture gets over, students line up in front of the library to get the reference books issued for a week. And that's it. This is the process followed day-by-day all through the year and at the end of it... The precious notebooks serve as a 'life saving boats' to swim across the three hour long examination.

This is the general picture of the higher education institutions, particularly Universities in our country.

The higher education institutions in India, particularly Universities, have fulfilled their responsibility of effectively transmitting the store of knowledge from one generation to another in the midst of political and social upheaval, social development and technological advancement till now, while remaining essentially unchanged in structure and method.

Will this proven model retain its resilience and relevance in the present century?

This era of radical and rapid change places demands on learners to increase their capacity for learning. This capacity is not necessarily about learning more, but about expanding and enhancing the ways in which learning takes place. There is the growing expectation that students should become more flexible, more self-reliant and autonomous, learners who can select personal pathways and who should develop the skills of lifelong learning. For fulfilling these expectations the learners have their own needs. In their higher education all of them need-

- Keen perception of new social trends and change.
- Skills of self-reliance, the ability to take, survive and profit from risks.
- Ability to develop and maintain value of their 'portfolio', to adapt goals in the face of changing circumstances and to seek out and manage and not to fear career transitions.
- Underlying confidence and sense of self-worth.
- Support towards responsibility in learning.

Thus, a sharper focus on being able to use knowledge and to use communication skills, collaboration and teamwork skills and thinking and decision making skills in both creating and using that knowledge is needed in preparing graduates for professional lives in the decades ahead.

In the changing world, the scenario of higher education is also changing. In India, there is Government –engineered expansion and renewed focus on higher education's contributions to society's skill base. At the sociological front, social forces in the last generation have radically changed the relative potency of the family for the socialization of prosocial values among the nation's youth. At the same time, the educational institutions include remarkably fewer opportunities for prosocial socialization of the students. In typical classrooms, students sit quietly and listen to the teachers hence, little prosocial socialization occurs. The consequence of this is the alarming increase in crimes against property within the educational institutions. Reports of theft, physical assault, student-student crimes have become extremely common. Students exhibit anti social behaviour. There is rise in drug abuse, bullying, violence and incivility.

Another consequence of the socialization void is the absence of cooperative skills among the students. Although students generally do not work cooperatively together within the campus, they are expected to do so when they leave the campus to enter the work force. The social structure within the educational institutions is out of synchrony with the social skill needs of our highly flexible technological economy. It is hard to point a job today that does not require cooperative interaction abilities. Around 70-80% of jobs today require "complex coordination of efforts and ideas".

The majority of the youth in India feels that because our education system is still based on the old paradigm of teaching and learning where knowledge is transferred from teacher to passive students, they lack in certain areas from their counterparts in other countries viz.

- Self-confidence
- Ability to uncover hidden opportunities
- Decision making abilities
- Networking skills
- Relevant experience
- Knowledge of social changes.

The phenomenon of globalization, the new mantra of 'collaboration', forming alliances and teams has created a need for interdisciplinary learning, the ability to cooperate with experts from other disciplines and work in conjugation. In present times, a sharper focus on being able to use knowledge and to use communication skills, teamwork skills, thinking and decision making skills in both creating and using that knowledge is needed in preparing graduates for professional lives. But somehow our education system lacks behind in providing these competencies to the students as by and large our system till secondary education level is still based on the old paradigm of teaching and learning, competitive interaction pattern is dominant, learning goals and performance goals are considered as two separate entities, there is over emphasis on cognitive goals which ensures development of talent but at the same time due to this productivity lags behind at the work place. This is due to the fact that students till secondary level of education imbibe the values propagated by competitive and individualistic learning. They imbibe the values of commitment of getting more than others, success depends on beating, defeating and getting more than others, what is important is winning not mastery or excellence and winning not learning is the goal of academic work.

The students become so self- centered that they lack in basic social skills, do not provide any support to others, do not cooperate with others and do not share their knowledge with others. Successful transition from academic life to work place requires that college graduates acquire field specific technical knowledge and professional skills of leadership, decision-making, trust-building, communication, and conflict-management skills. Professional education faculty members are today challenged to design pedagogy that explicitly teaches and rewards student development of professional skills crucial for work place success.

Time has come when Higher education may have to respond to the opportunistic, flexible, pro-active approaches to learning which modern social activity and lifestyles represent.

Considering the present scenario, where educators are faced with a number of issues that concern ensuring that educational institutions are "world class", it has now become a necessity that we adopt instructional practices which are in congruence with the present times. Cooperative Learning is one such method.

Twenty first century living is characterized by global, interdependent communities and by complex social institutions that require high degree of cooperation among members. Without the cooperation of its members society cannot survive. In an industrial organization also, it's the group effort that counts. There's really no room for stars in an industrial organization. Consequently, most people prize cooperative behaviour and believe it to be an important goal for education.

Cooperative learning researchers and practitioners have shown that positive peer relationships are essential to success in college. Isolation and alienation are the best predictors of failure. Two major reasons for dropping out of college are failure to establish a social network of friends and classmates, and failure to become academically involved in classes. Working together with fellow students, solving problems together, and talking through material together has other benefits as well. Student participation, teacher encouragement, and student-student interaction positively relate to improved critical thinking. These three activities confirm other research and theory stressing the importance of active practice, motivation, and feedback in thinking skills as well as other skills.

An important aspect of psychological health is social competence. Social skills and competencies tend to increase more within cooperative than in competitive or individualistic situations. Working together to get the job done increases student's ability to provide leadership, build and maintain trust, communicate effectively and manage conflicts constructively thus, promoting higher self esteem.

So it seems that cooperative experiences in the campus are the only viable way to systematically socialize future generations to meet the needs presented by an increasingly urban, technological, and interdependent world.

AT TEACHER EDUCATION LEVEL

If teachers are not taught to cooperate in their teacher education programs, it is difficult to learn. If teachers are not afforded opportunities to cooperate, it is difficult to practice. Working in isolation becomes a habit. The way the majority of teacher education programs are structured in India today, few, if any, allow opportunities for pre-service teacher trainees to cooperate with one another. From this training, educators are taught they do not need to cooperate with one another. The unspoken message is they do not need to know what the other is doing. This is a dangerous message that is then carried out into public school classrooms by in-service teachers as the same culture is present once the teacher trainees reach the classroom. Rarely are elementary and secondary teachers afforded the opportunity to work cooperatively with one another. They have much to learn from one another in terms of curriculum, theory, and practice, yet they are left to function competitively and individualistically instead of cooperatively. Such training fosters working competitively and individualistically over cooperatively (*Johnson* and *Johnson*, 1988). The reverse is true for any school or educational setting. Cooperation exists and is needed within any educational setting at each and every level. There ought to be cooperation between principal and teachers, between teachers, between teachers and students and between students as well. No competition can occur if there is no cooperation on rules, procedures, time, place and criteria for determining the winner. Skills and information learned individualistically have to be enacted within a social system. Teachers trained through only competitive and individualistic learning structures imbibe the values of competition and individualization within themselves and pass it on as it is to their students. This process has been going on since a long time and everyone has been overlooking the third dimension of structuring a learning situation.

As teachers, it is our job to help children grow into the intellectual life around them. In order to do so, the teachers must model what they want the students to imitate. In essence, we must practice what we preach. If we want our students to take an active role in cooperative learning, we must examine how we model cooperative learning in our own school lives.

Cooperative Learning should be included in the teacher training programme with the intention to offer opportunities to teacher trainees to develop a sense of community ethos and at the same time accountability and to establish an emotional bond through trust to enable success and learning for all participants. The sense of belonging, working together, taking risks and encouraging each other during cooperative learning activities help sensitize teacher trainees towards this unused alternative. Cooperative learning experiences when integrated into their training programme offer particular means for teacher trainees to work together to attain the best that they collectively can. Effective teacher preparation requires that participants develop a sense of community. The longevity of relationships required to establish community has several advantages for all of its members. It brings coherence to programs, fosters an appreciation of the power of cooperative effort, and encourages a dialogue that promotes the continual rejuvenation of teacher education. Consequently, all of our teacher education programs must foster a sense of community among their students, among faculty members, between faculty members and students, and between the university and the schools. Effective teachers reflect critically on the moral, political, social, and economic dimensions of education. This requires an understanding of the multiple contexts in which schools function, an appreciation of diverse perspectives on educational issues, and a commitment to democratic forms of interaction. Consequently, all of our teacher education programs must encourage students to develop their own social and educational visions that are connected to critically reflective practice. Teachers who are more than technicians or mere purveyors of information must be committed to lifelong intellectual, personal, and professional growth. Both faculty and students must continually develop these habits of mind, requiring that our programs stimulate the exploration and development of the full range of human capabilities. Consequently, all of our teacher education programs must foster intellectual curiosity and encourage an appreciation of learning through intuition, imagination, cooperation and aesthetic experience. Teachers must be effective in actual educational settings. Accordingly, our teacher education programs must maintain or create experiences in schools and on campus that will assist in the development of their expertise in those settings. Students should be expected to act as thoughtful, reflective, caring practitioners as part of those experiences, and instructors must be able to assess their abilities in such settings. Consequently, all of our teacher education programs must include early and continuous engagement—through direct immersion or simulation—with the multiple realities of children, teaching, and schools. Effective teachers possess a well-grounded knowledge of the content areas that are central to their teaching. They also have an in-depth comprehension of the forms of knowledge embodied in the traditional disciplines, of the interdisciplinary nature of inquiry, and of the multiple forms of understanding that individual students bring to the classroom. Consequently all of our teacher education programs must help students acquire a 'practical wisdom' that integrates forms of understanding, skilled action in and outside classrooms, and a particular sensitivity to the diversity of students. Good teachers build on their students' interests, learning styles, and goals. Similarly, teacher education should offer its students opportunities to individualize and personalize their preparation as teachers in the community context. Consequently, all of our teacher education programs must give students a significant measure of control over how, when, and where their learning takes place, thus enabling their interests and values to shape major portions of their work. Teacher education courses offer new experiences and different demands. Teacher trainees must be able to demonstrate skills, competencies and dispositions in performance assessments. Cooperative groups offer such opportunities to them. A sense of "*we are all in it together*" translates to "*together we can do it.*" The elements of cooperative learning viz. positive interdependence, individual accountability, social skill development and intercommunication and group processing in itself, seem a viable reason to incorporate cooperative learning into teacher education programme.

The realization of Quality Education, to a great extent, depends on quality of teachers injected into the educational system. Quality of teachers, in turn, depends on the general and professional education teachers receive before entering the profession and the extent to which they develop on the job. The need for lifelong education and training is now universally acknowledged in all walks of life, but it is doubly relevant to teaching. Hence, we should include academic interventions which cater to such needs in our Teacher Education programme.

CONCLUSION

Out of the three domains of reforms in our education system namely- structure, content and process, the process reforms in our education system are practically conspicuous by their absence. The change, if any, is so imperceptible that the area looks stagnant. The stereotype teacher training programmes keep on producing teachers with indifferent professional attitudes. The pathetic state of process reform in teacher education is equally reflected in the process reforms in schools which are equally discouraging. The orientation and refresher courses offered to the in-service teachers at primary and secondary level and even at higher education level by the concerned agencies stick to the conventional methods. Despite policy statements to foster creativity, positive interdependence, independent thinking, individual accountability, variety of study skills, social skills, initiative and positive attitudes, the process of teaching remains as unresponsive to these objectives and individual needs as it used to be in the past. In such a situation, with no other alternative, one looks helplessly to the stagnating textbook and examination enslavement of teachers and teaching. There is little wonder that the system produces highly dependent students- dependent on teachers, dependent on textbooks and readymade answer guides. Only infinitesimally small and accomplished young persons with initiative sustain and emerge out from this stereotype culture. It is true that without process reform in teaching and learning we cannot broad base our academic excellence. We can ignore it at our own peril.

Should we suffer from the paralytic stroke of pessimism or should we analyze the malaise in the education system, search ways to meet the challenge and implement the programme to change the process of training teachers to ensure change in the process of teaching to achieve a variety of objectives? The latter is the obvious action-oriented choice to ensure really educated future generations with thinking minds.

In teaching and training the greatest challenge is to inspire teachers and teacher educators to professional excellence. (*Ruben*, 1989). It means that training should foster in teachers the ability to match teaching to learning styles of students and instructional objectives. It also includes the ability to adapt to the teaching situation in different learning environments and individual needs of heterogeneous group of learners in classroom. An effective teacher is one who has acquired the necessary capabilities to operationalize instructional skills, identify learning styles of students, select appropriate instructional procedures and strategies for presenting the content using appropriate media and take relevant decisions affecting a match among these variables. He is also required to take classroom management decisions. This is what has been outlined as pedagogical intelligence. The greatest weakness of the present training programmes is the failure to develop capability in teachers to take such decisions because of their enslavement to curriculum, textbook and examination. In teacher education programmes, teacher trainees are taught about the theories of Piaget and Vygotsky but never trained how to put the worth of Zone of Proximal development to practice in classrooms. The result is ineffective training and teaching. The poor children are the silent victims. The student initiative, the joy of learning and the drive for excellence are killed before these can bloom in the individuals who come to our institutions for learning. Only effective teaching can ameliorate the suffering community of students. At the higher education level also the orientation courses are unsuccessful in driving the lecturers and professors towards the pedagogical intelligence. They adopt the same stereotype method which their predecessors adopted while teaching them and with which they feel quite comfortable.

There is clear need to include academic interventions such as Cooperative Learning in our educational programmes. *John I. Goodlad's* (1990) 10th postulate among the nineteen he considers important for creating quality education programmes is call for teachers and educators to model best practices in their classrooms. Based on the strong foundation of different theoretical perspectives on learning viz. social interdependence theory (*Kurt Lewin and Morton Deutsch*), cognitive developmental psychology (*Jean Piaget, Lev Vygotsky*) and behavioral-social perspective (*Skinner*)- Cooperative Learning is one such strategy which has all the required ingredients to empower the education system. Cooperative Learning has been found to enhance student achievement, encourage positive self esteem and facilitate growth in social interaction skills (*Johnson* and *Johnson*, 1991; *Kagan*, 1989, 1990; *Slavin*, 1991). For such practices to be more widely disseminated and to prepare highly qualified teachers, schools and colleges of education must make such practice a routine part of their preparation efforts. Academic staff colleges should also include it in their orientation and refresher courses. Cooperative learning strategies can be and should be used with teacher candidates to improve their own knowledge and skills, model the use of such strategies with students and document the impact that candidates have on pupil learning.

Research findings indicate positive outcomes associated with cooperative learning. Although past history emphasized individualism, the future will be marked by more cooperative efforts. The role of a teacher is interconnected with the benefits of cooperative learning. These roles involve creating classrooms conditions in which students are given freedom to become active students, construct meaning, think critically, find relationships, clarify thinking and respond to challenges. Cooperative learning, by its very nature, invites students to become active learners. New perspectives are shared within groups as a result of the existing variety of background knowledge. Listening skills are honed as students read, report and communicate ideas to each other and engage in problem solving as a group. Generalizations are supported by facts that students obtain by returning to the text for verification, thus, clarifying ideas. Students not only learn by teaching, analyzing and synthesizing information, but also develop social skills in a less threatening atmosphere. Small groups demand a degree of metacognitive awareness by which students constantly monitor their statements and progress toward a goal.

There is a volume of research based findings regarding the benefits realized as a result of cooperative learning. (*Johnson* and *Johnson*, 1989, 1991; *Kagan*, 1989, 1991; *Sharan* and *Sharan*, 1989, 1990; *Slavin*, 1989, 1990, 1991). The research indicates that if student-student interdependence is structured carefully and appropriately, students will achieve at a higher level, more frequently use higher-level reasoning strategies, have higher levels of achievement motivation, be more intrinsically motivated, develop more positive interpersonal relationships with each other, value more the subject area being studied, have higher self-esteem, and be more skilled interpersonally.

The research covers the full range of subject areas and age levels and has been available for some time. In light of such findings, it seems logical to expect cooperative learning to be both exemplified and taught in our education programmes. It is not difficult to prepare educators to select the appropriate goal structure for an instructional activity, implement it so that a certain student-student interaction pattern is achieved, and then instruct students in the social skills they need to interact appropriately and effectively with each other. It is time we did so because-

"*What the child can do in cooperation today he can do alone tomorrow.*" (*Vygotsky*, 1986, p.188)

David and *Roger Johnson* (1985) also claimed that despite the documented effectiveness of cooperative learning, this teaching strategy has received little attention. *Lawrence Lyman* and *Harvey Foyle* (1990) declared that it was "......lamentable that there are still colleges of education that graduate teachers and principals who are not equipped with the skills necessary for effective collaboration and cooperation" (p.12). They insisted that the skills necessary to implement interactive methods such as Cooperative Learning be included in every teacher education programme. *Allan Glatthorn* (1993) cautioned beginning teachers that a pre requisite to the successful implementation of cooperative learning was systematic instruction about this complex model. Many of the teachers model or teach the way they were taught – by lecturing. But research has shown that after fifteen to twenty minutes of lecture a student stops listening or paying attention (*Tileston*, 2000). To counteract the loss in interest, Cooperative learning can be practiced and emphasized during each class. So, if future teachers are to make positive use of cooperative learning, they need to know what it is, recognize the value of the strategy and have knowledge and skill to plan cooperative learning activities. Therefore, teacher educators face the challenge of how best to ensure that pre-service teachers and lecturers are taught using cooperative learning so as to sensitize them and make them aware of the power and value of the strategy, help them to acquire the knowledge and skill required to enable them to implement cooperative learning and at the same time influence them to want to learn to use the model.

The importance of cooperative learning goes much beyond maximizing outcomes such as achievement, positive attitudes toward subject areas, and the ability to think critically, although these are worthwhile outcomes. The elements of cooperative learning viz. teamwork through positive interdependence, communication, effective coordination, and division of labour by exhibiting individual accountability are keystones which characterize most real-life settings. The same is true about our schools as school is considered to be a miniature society. It is time for schools to reflect the reality of adult life. Incorporating cooperative learning experiences in the classroom will both reinforce the skills necessary to cope with future courses and provide students with the qualifications that will make them employable. Supporting the development of these skills is the teacher, who is no longer the dispenser of knowledge, but the guide, the challenger, the listener, the encourager, the learner.

For according to *Moffet* (1983), "The role of the teacher is to teach students to teach each other". (p.196).

The most logical way to ensure that students master the cooperative skills required in most task-oriented situations is to structure the majority of academic learning situations cooperatively. For this to become a reality we will have to train our teachers through cooperative learning because only when they experience beneficial changes within them they will be able to realize the value of cooperative learning and will get the urge and strength from within to break-free from the enslavement of competitive and individualistic learning. It will improve their teaching effectiveness drastically as they would acquire skills and intelligentsia to pass on the legacy they have received. For such practices to be more widely disseminated and to prepare highly qualified teachers, schools and colleges of education, academic staff colleges and other agencies must make such practice a routine part of their preparation efforts. Cooperative learning strategies can be and should be used with teacher candidates to improve their own knowledge and skills, model the use of such strategies with students and document the impact that teachers have on pupil learning. These neophyte teachers subconsciously believe that giving lectures must be the way to teach as they are most familiar with the same. This mentality must change. If teachers are going to incorporate cooperative strategies in their teaching, they must learn via cooperative strategies. Cooperative learning has proven itself useful in defusing tensions in a classroom through the focus on interpersonal communication and the development of social skills. (*Johnson et al*, 1990). It seems natural that future teachers should have this technique in their personal array of teaching tools.

As the Chinese proverb suggests:

"When I hear I forget, When I see I remember, When I do I learn."

Adults and children learn by "doing" and it makes sense that instructors need to offer opportunities for students to participate in cooperative learning tasks.

Bibliography

Artzt, A. and Newman, C. (1990), How to Use Cooperative Learning in the Mathematics Class. Reston,VA: National Council of Teachers of Mathematics.

Caroselli, M.(1998). Great Session Openers, Closers and Energizers. New York:McGraw-Hill.

Coleman, D. (1995). Emotional Intelligence: Why it can Matter More Than IQ. New York: Bantam Books.

Cowie, H. & Rudduck, J. (1988) School and Classroom Studies. London: BP Educational Service.

Davidson, N. (Ed.) (1990), Cooperative Learning in Mathematics: A Handbook for Teachers, Menlo Park: Addison Wesley.

Deutsch, M. (1949). A Theory of Cooperation and Competition. Human Relations, 2, 129-152.

Felder, R. (1997). Cooperative Learning in a Sequence of Engineering Courses: A Success Story. Cooperative Learning and College Teaching Newsletter, 5(2), pp. 10-13.

Gardner. (1983). Frames of Mind. New York: Basic Books.

Glatthorn, A. (1993). Learning Twice: An Introduction to the Methods of Teaching. New York: Harper Collins Publishers.

Goodlad, J. (1990). Better Teachers for Our Nations Schools. Phi Delta Kappan, 72 (3), pp. 184-194.

Goodsell, A., Maher, M., and Tinto, V. (1992), Collaborative Learning: A Sourcebook for Higher Education, University Park, PA: National Center on Postsecondary Teaching, Learning and Assessment.

Graves, D. (1983). Writing: Teachers and Children at Work. Exeter, NH: Heinemann.

Hertz-Lazarowitz, R., Kirkus, V., Miller, N., (1992) "An Overview of the Theoretical Anatomy of Cooperation in the Classroom" in Hertz-Lazarowitz Ed. Interaction in Cooperative Groups: The Theoretical Anatomy of Group Learning NY, NY: Cambridge University Press, pp. 3-4.

Johnson, D.W. (1970). Social Psychology of Education. Edina, MN: Interaction Book Company.

Johnson, D.W. (1979). Educational Psychology. Englewood Cliffs, NJ: Prentice Hall.

Johnson, D.W., Johnson, R.T., Holubec, E.J., (1988, 1992, 1998), Advanced Cooperative Learning- Revised. Edina, MN: Interaction Book Co.

Johnson D.W. and Johnson R.T. (1989). Cooperation and Competition Theory and Research. Edina, MN: Interaction Book Company.

Johnson, D.W., & Johnson, R.T. (1974). Instructional Goal Structure: Cooperative, Competitive, Or Individualistic. Review of Educational Research, 44, pp. 213-240.

Johnson, D.W. and Johnson, R.T. (1979). Conflict in the Classroom: Controversy and Learning. Review of Educational Research, 49, pp. 51-61.

Johnson, R.T., and Johnson, D.W. (1988).Cooperative Learning: Two Heads Learn Better Than One. Edina, MN: Interaction Book Co.

Johnson D.W. and Johnson R.T. (1989). Cooperation and Competition Theory and Research. Edina, MN: Interaction Book Co.

Johnson, D.W. and Johnson, R.T. (1989). Cooperative Learning Methods: A Meta-Analysis. The Newsletter of the Cooperative Learning Institute, 15(1), February 2000.

Johnson, D.W. and Johnson, R.T. (1991). Learning Together and Alone. (3rd ed.). Englewood Cliffs, NJ: Prentice Hall.

Johnson, D.W., Johnson, R.T., and Smith, K. (1991). Cooperative Learning: Increasing College Faculty Instructional Productivity, ASHE-ERIC Higher Education Report No. 4, Washington, DC: The George Washington University.

Johnson, D.W. and Johnson, R.T. (1992), "Encouraging Thinking Through Constructive Controversy", in Davidson and Worsham (Eds.) Enhancing Thinking Through Cooperative Learning, NY, NY: College Teachers Press.

Johnson, D.W., Johnson, R.T., Holubec, E.J., (1984). Cooperation in the Classroom. Edina, MN: Interaction Book Co.

Johnson,D.W, Johnson,R.T. and Smith, K. (1986). Academic Conflict Among Students: Controversy And Learning. In R. Feldman (Ed.), The Social Psychology of Education. Cambridge: Cambridge University Press, pp. 199-231.

Johnson, D.W., Johnson, R.T. and Holubec,E. (1998). Cooperation in the Classroom. (Revised Edition) Boston: Allyn and Bacon.

Johnson, R.T., and Johnson, D.W. (1988). Cooperative Learning: Two Heads Learn Better Than One. Edina, MN: Interaction Book Co.

Kagan, S. (1990). Constructive Controversy. Cooperative Learning, 10(3), 20-26.

Kagan S., (1990). Cooperative Learning: Resources for Teachers. San Juan Capistrano, CA: Resources for Teachers.

Kagan S. and Kagan M. (1992). Advanced Cooperative Learning: Playing with Elements. San Juan Capistrano, CA: Kagan Cooperative Learning.

Kohn, A. (1992). Resistance to Cooperative Learning: Making Sense of its Deletion and Dilution. Journal of Education, 174(2), 38-56.

Lyman, L. and Foyle, H. (1990). Cooperative Grouping for Interactive Learning: Students, Teachers and Administrators. Washington, DC: National Education Association.

Marzano, R.J., (1992), The Many Faces of Cooperation Across The Dimensions of Learning, in Davidson & Worsham (Eds.), Enhancing Thinking Through Cooperative Learning, NY, NY: Teachers College Press, pp. 20-31.

Moffet, J. (1994). Getting Freshman Started Right. Presentation at the Annual Meting on the Ohio Association for Developmental Education, Portsmouth, OH.

Montagu, A. (1965). The Human Revolution. New York: World Pub Co.

Nelson-LeGall, S., (1992) "Children's instrumental help-seeking. It's role in the social acquisition and construction of knowledge", in Lazarowitz Ed. Interaction in Cooperative groups: Theoretical Anatomy of Group Learning, New York: Cambridge University Press, pp.120-141.

Sharan, S. (1990). Cooperative Learning: Theory and Research. Westport, CT: Praeger Publishers.

Sharan, S. (Ed.) (1999). Handbook of Cooperative Learning Methods. Westport, CT: Praeger.

Sharan, Y. and Sharan, S. (1989-1990). Group Investigation Expands Cooperative Learning. Educational Leadership, 47(4), 17-21.

Slavin R.E. (1990). Cooperative Learning: Theory, Research and Practice. Englewood Cliffs, NJ: Prentice Hall.

Slavin, R.E. (1991). Synthesis of Research of Cooperative Learning. Educational Leadership, 48,71-82.

Slavin, RE. (1992). When and why does cooperative learning increase achievement? Theoritical and empirical perspectives. In R. Hertz-Lazarowitz and N. Milier (eds.), Interaction in cooperative: The theoretical anatomy of group learning. New York: Cambridge University Press, pp. 145-173.

Slavin, R.E. (1995). Cooperative Learning: Theory, Research and Practice, (2nd Ed.) Boston: Allyn and Bacon.

Slavin, R.E. (1995). Cooperative Learning. (2nd Ed.). Massachussetts: Allyn and Bacon.

Staub, E. (2002). From Healing Past Wounds to the Development of Inclusive Caring: Contents and Processes of Peace Education. In G. Salomon and B. Nevo (Eds.),

Peace education: The concept, principles, and practices around the world. Mahwah, NJ: Erlbaum, pp. 73-86.

Stenberg. (1985). Beyond IQ: A Triarchic Theory of Human Intelligence. Cambridge: Cambridge University Press.

Tileston, D.W. (2000). 10 Best Teaching Practices: How Brain Research, Learning Styles and Standards Define Teaching Competencies, California:Corwin Press.

Tinto, V. (1997). Enhancing Learning Via Community. Thought and Action, 13(1), 53-58.

Vygotsky, L. (1962). Thought and Language. Cambridge, MA: MIT Press.

Vygotsky, L. (1978). Mind in Society: The Development of Higher Psychological Processes, Cambridge, Massachusetts: Harvard University Press.

Vygotsky, L. (1986). Thought and Language. (4th ed.) Cambridge, MA: Harvard University Press.

Index

D

U

V

Z